YOUNG CALVIN IN PARIS,

AND

THE LITTLE FLOCK THAT HE FED.

BY THE

REV. WM. M. BLACKBURN,

AUTHOR OF

"THE REBEL PRINCE," "JUDAS THE MACCOABEE,"
"THE EXILES OF MADEIRA," &c.

PHILADELPHIA:
PRESBYTERIAN BOARD OF PUBLICATION,
No. 821 CHESTNUT STREET.

STEREOTYPED BY WESTCOTT & THOMSON.

PREFACE.

THE warp and the woof of this volume are facts drawn from history and biography; the surface colours are partly supplied by imagination. In its preparation several works have been consulted, but chiefly D'Aubignè's "History of the Reformation in the time of Calvin." It is intended to follow "The College Days of Calvin."

If it shall lead the young reader to study the history of the Reformation, and, especially, to cherish the true faith of the martyrs, the author will be rewarded for the pleasant work of a few stormy days.

W. M. B.

TRENTON, N. J.

CONTENTS.

CHAPTER VIII.

CHAPTER IX.

CHAPTER X.

YOUNG CALVIN IN PARIS.

CHAPTER I.

MADNESS FOR IMAGES.

MORE than three hundred years ago, there lived in Paris a poor waterman, who kept his little boat on the river Seine. One day, in June, 1528, a stranger took a seat on the bench, saying,

"Do not wait for any one else, but row me across in a hurry."

The boatman wanted to wait for more passengers, but plied his oar and thought that he was carrying a student to the Latin Quarter, on the southern side of the river, almost opposite the Cathedral of Notre-Dame. The stranger sang a coarse song in ridicule of the monks, and the waterman gazed at him, and was charmed with his round musical voice. Perhaps a more handsome young man had never sat in the little boat.

"How do you like that?" said the stranger, after the vulgar chorus was ended.

"I do not like the words, but I admire the music."

"Perhaps you would like this," said the flattered singer, and he began a song to the Virgin Mary, in which she was adored as "the mother of God, the queen of heaven, the mediatress of men, and the refuge of sinners."

"No, that does not please me," said the boatman, who wished he could take back his words, as soon as they were gone from his lips. The poor man betrayed his fears.

"Do not fear me," said the singer. "If you were the man who broke the heads off the images of Our Lady and her child, I would not tell the gang of officers who are searching all the houses in the city. Not I; you may trust me for that, because they were very insolent at my home, and ransacked every nook where a man could hide. The whole city was running mad after such images, and I am glad that some one has broken the statue that so many worshipped in the quarter of St. Antoine. Did they search your house?"

"Indeed they did, and it's a poor little hut that nobody could hide in. And they took——." The boatman thought it unwise to finish the sentence.

"Took what? your money? You need not be so cautious."

"Something far better than money. Since you seem to be so friendly, I must tell you it was my Testament. They carried it off, and next, I shall be seized."

"So you are a heretic; very well, you know what

to expect. You will be burned, if you trouble yourself with such books; and that is all the consolation I can give you, unless you will send me word when your hour is coming, and let me look on when you are at the stake. Perhaps you will recant, though."

"No, sir: I cannot deny my Master. I have one brand on my forehead now, and it is only a little mark that the good Shepherd puts on his straying sheep."

"Let me see." The waterman lifted his slouched hat, and the stranger came near to see how deep the hot iron had burned into the poor man's forehead. "Horrible, cruel tyrants," he exclaimed, adding much more in a profaner strain.

"Hold, my friend," said the branded ferryman, in a soft tone. "Let us forgive our enemies, and pray for them that persecute us. I thank them, for ever since that trial of my faith, I have been a happier man."

"Where was the brand put upon you?"

"At Meaux, where the good Lefevre printed the New Testament and Farel preached to us until he was driven away. We had happy times there while the bishop favoured us, but alas! they frightened him and he recanted, and then it was a sad day for us. Beda went there from Paris, and he scattered the flock."

"And so you have come right here where the terrible Beda lives—he has his quarters right over there near the Old Sorbonne. Be careful or he will find you out. He has his pack everywhere, ferretting out and hounding down all who read your Testament. I hate him; I hate his religion, but he don't burn people like me. I wish I had to make his boots for him; if I did not make them pinch and pierce his feet, then I am not a shoemaker."

The boatman looked with increased interest at the stranger, as they touched the bank. Who could he be? Could not such an independent young man be converted to the truth? He must speak a word to him. He gently said, "Friend, let a poor *Christaudin* beg of you to get a Testament and read it."

"If I could get one for you, I would gladly replace what has been stolen from you, but I will not read it. I choose to live a gay life. If I am not too drunk, or do not get beaten in a fray, I will be master at a merry dance to-night. I am a free fellow, and the priests do not think me a heretic, for I used to pay them well at mass just to keep up a fair show. It is all nonsense. I will not be a hypocrite; if there is any true religion, you have it. Be true to it; you will be worth burning, and, no doubt, you will be happy in the flames. I know you have something in your heart that you want to tell me; but it's no use. Here is your fare." He seemed to treat money with as much levity as he did the most serious subjects.

"Not so much as this by half, sir," said the boatman, holding out his hand to give back part of the coin.

"Keep it all. Buy you a Testament and be happy. If you wish to favour me, I'll tell you how to do it. Be here at midnight and take me back."

"I never run my boat so late as that."

"You shall have double pay. And if you want to know my name, it is Berthelot Milon. My father is a shoemaker in St. Martin street, between the two law courts. Never call me Bartholomew, for that is the name of a Saint's day."

"You may depend upon me," said the waterman, partly persuaded by his need of money and bread, and partly by the hope of talking again with the noblest looking young man that he had ever seen walking away toward the college in the Latin quarter. He stood gazing after Berthelot, now fearing that he had said too much, and now wishing that he had said more.

Presently there came four officers leading a man in chains. They looked at his boat, said it was too small, took a larger one and started for the other side. One glance at the prisoner told our boatman who he was. He had often carried him over, and they had rowed slowly and had many a pleasant talk. He was a student, whom the great and good Berquin supported at college. He had refused to join the procession of five hundred students, and the scores of professors, doctors, licentiates and friars, who marched to the spot where the image of Mary had been broken on the night of Whitsunday. He felt opposed to such idolatry, and did not think that

Beautiful it was to see
Such a goodly company,
Monks gray, black, of every hue,
Walking for an hour or two.

He must be put in prison until he could give a reason for his conduct, for perhaps he had a hand in mutilating the image. "I wish he had not been across the river so late, on the night that the statue was broken," said the waterman to himself, as he thought how his innocent friend might be put to death.

Then came a stranger, who took a seat in his boat, and he pushed it off with his oar.

"They have at last seized the man who wrought the wicked mischief, I hope," said the stranger. "He ought to die this very hour, for such an injury to 'the glorious Mother of God.'"

The pious boatman was shocked to hear such language, which was then very common in Paris. The passenger continued to extol the "glorious mother" in the highest terms, and taking out a picture of Mary, he offered it to his carrier. The poor man was rowing with all his might; he suddenly stopped, took the picture, and, with a horror of images and of the blasphemies uttered, he tore it to pieces, and threw the fragments into the water, saying sharply, "The Virgin Mary has no more power than that bit of paper." The stranger burned with rage, but said not a word; as soon as he was landed he ran to inform the officers of what had occurred. Perhaps this was the man whom the police had been eagerly seeking.

We will not follow Berthelot Milon through all the scenes of the day, when he drank wine with the students, sang vulgar songs for lounging priests at the taverns, strolled about with company too bad for us to describe, and passed the evening with the lowest class of dancers at a ball which needed the attention of the detective police. At midnight the revelry was high, but he sought his hat. Evil associates wondered and begged him to linger, but he broke away from their grasp. The poor waterman was in his thoughts, and he must see him again, yet he scarcely knew for what reason. He came to the landing; the little boat was not there. He waited, refused to go with others who were crossing, sat down, rose again, paced to and fro, made inquiries, learned nothing, at last got angry. "The fellow has been false to his promise," said he. Then thinking of the student he had seen, that morning, in chains, he said, "No; he has been arrested. The wolves have dragged him to their den." He took the next boat, crossed the river, and hastened home.

"Well, my son," said his father, who looked up from his shoe-bench when he saw Berthelot enter the shop, "I did my work by daylight, and now I am doing yours. What will Surgeon Pointet say if these shoes are not done at nine this morning, for it is morning now?"

"I'll finish them: you please retire." He felt

touched at seeing his kind father toiling until such late hours.

"Your mother has been coming and going all night, in great distress, lest you should be brought home drunk and sorely beaten, or perhaps dead. Have you no mercy on your parents?"

"So he has come home at last," said the mother, entering the shop, which was a front room in the house. She came near, looked to see if his eyes were blackened, and said, "You have been drinking, but I am glad you are so nearly sober."

He told where he had been, and ended by saying, "If I thought that poor waterman was in the great prison, I would go and break open the doors and bring him out."

"Folly, all folly," exclaimed Robert, his father. "You set yourself up against the Sorbonne to rescue heretics! You think you could oppose the holy church, do you? May no son of mine ever be so rash. Remember the Grève does not get cool very often in these times, when the holy church must deal justly with these gospellers."

"Yes; holy church, indeed! Have I not seen her good monks and priests carousing this very night?"

"Not all of them. You did not see friar Bernard, nor others like him among them."

"Very true; your confessor, friar Bernard, is one of the best of the clergy, but he will never win me to his faith. I know this city better than you do;

perhaps I know it too well; and somehow it happens that these poor gospellers are a harmless, excellent sort of people. I know they are heretics, and I hate their heresy; I know that they sin against holy church by not adoring the Virgin Mary, and yet I wish they would dash in pieces every image that she has in all Paris. If she is so powerful why does she not protect her statues? If she destroys those who break them, then why is the Sorbonne so busy hunting for the man who severed the head from the one in St. Antoine? He must be dead already. Yet you allow the officers to insult you, and suspect you, and search through all your house."

"But after wearying and worrying ourselves up to this hour, for your sake, we will hardly allow you to insult us. We will leave you till daylight, and then you will have soberer thoughts," said Robert Milon, all of which was true enough, by the time Surgeon Pointet called to get his shoes.

Berthelot was quite drowsy when the Surgeon came, but he roused himself up by pouring forth his ridicule against the monks. "I am quite of your mind," said Pointet, "for I came to Paris with a great reverence for them. But I have 'doctored' them up long enough to find them out. They are mostly a set of diseased debauchees. I see that the gospel is not among them; I must look for it somewhere else."

"Let it alone, as I do," replied Berthelot, who

would have been a thorough French revolutionist, if he had lived two hundred and fifty years later. He wished to see all religion put away from France, and liberty, equality, and mirth established.

"I am beginning to read the Bible, my young friend," said the Surgeon, "and let me urge you to do likewise. If all the people would read it, the church would soon be reformed."

Berthelot refused to open the New Testament. He knew that it would teach him the need of a more moral life, and he wished no restraints to be put upon his conscience or his conduct. His friend left, and he went to a breakfast which proved to him the providence of a mother's love. He felt ashamed of the way in which he had spent the previous day, and yet he went on spending many other days in the same manner. Often did he stroll down to the river to see if the waterman could be found.

A few weeks had passed, when he was at work on his bench, and suddenly heard a great clangour of the bells of Notre Dame. "A heretic is going to the stake," said he, "and I will run and see him." He was soon in front of the Old Cathedral of "Our Lady," (Notre Dame,) but finding no procession there, he rushed on to the public square called the Gréve. Doctors and monks were there in abundance, and a great crowd of people. At length the archers came, and the cart with the victim in it. "It is the waterman," said Berthelot, with intense excitement, starting forward through the guards. Lances were raised, bows were drawn, orders were given to arrest him, but he escaped the blows that would have levelled him, and shouted, "You are burning an innocent man."

"Strike him down," cried an officer. The guards seemed only to strike each other. The order was changed, "hold, hold!" for they were as likely to wound the prisoner as Berthelot. If they should kill the waterman, they could not have the pleasure of burning him.

"Do you know me?" asked Berthelot, as he seized the hand of the Christaudin. "Those boat-songs—do you remember?"

"Surely I do," and they fell into each other's arms. The guards dared not interfere, for the people were almost ready to rise up against them, and rescue the prisoner, and what was best of all was friar Bernard was in the cart.

"Did you think that I had anything to do in your arrest?" said Berthelot.

"I now am sure you had not; pardon me for having had a little suspicion of you. I am glad that I can die with this awful thought off my mind."

"I can't release you from this horrible death; can I do anything to comfort you?"

"I die happy. I am only stepping into my chariot of fire. But if I could hear that full round voice again!"—

"You shall hear it, if I am not killed on the spot.

Listen at the right time." They pressed each other's lips, and clung hand in hand together, until forced to separate. The awful ceremonies were performed; the Christian seemed to forget the injustice of the charges read against him, and employed all his last breath in telling the people of that Saviour who was crucified for them. The fire was kindled, the martyr felt its horrors, and amid the groans of the crowd, he could hear one clear voice singing aloud to cheer him, and the last sight he had in this world, was that of the noblest face which, that day, was almost blistered by the flames. The words were improvised; the tune led the officers to think that it was a song to the Virgin Mary. Friar Bernard knew better, but he was secretly rejoicing in the firm faith of the Christian, who was put to death because he would not adore the excellent Mother of Jesus as equally glorious with her divine Son.

The artless boatman was probably deceived, with the idea that Berthelot had read the Testament and become a true believer. There was no piety in his breast; nothing but a heroic hatred of cruelty and a pity for the sufferer. Yet the martyr's prayer must have risen for his friend. Would that prayer ever be answered?

Berthelot was the ring-leader of too large a number of young men to fail of winning admiration. They gathered about him on the streets, they flattered him in the shop, they made suppers for him at the taverns, and they cheered him for his wit, his vulgar songs, and his bold speeches. "A clever fellow with a big heart;" they said, "he breaks off from us the shackles of the priests, and teaches us how to be free and how to enjoy life." His head was completely turned; he dreamed of raising up a party of young men who would be able to rush forth and stop the burning of a man on the Grève, just as a fire-company would quench the flames of a house on fire.

"Go on, Berthelot," they shouted; "you are safe. The Bedists will not burn you, for they know that you live too freely and loosely ever to be a heretic. Only righteous men are put to death; rakes are kindly spared."

"Yes; but every one of you deserves the rod; you know it. You make fools of yourselves just because I do;" Berthelot would reply, for he delighted in lecturing them occasionally, in order to soothe his own conscience and to hold their respect. "You must not go too far. You must make it appear beautiful and enticing to lead our kind of a life, Keep an eye on every young man who comes to Paris. Cultivate him; whisper of the liberal ideas, and if he loves free-thinking and free-living, draw him into our band."

It was often said that Berthelot knew everybody, and that everybody in his quarter talked about him and his exploits. Some spoke with admiration, others with fear. He equally courted pleasures and quarrels, and rushed into a strife as soon as any discussion arose, nor did he often cease his fray until he was the proud victor. His impulses led him to do some of the best and some of the worst of human deeds.

CHAPTER II.

A NEW STATUE.

"WELL, I've got rid of that monk again; he must suppose I am worth a great deal of attention. I'll tell him next time what I think of his religion. Perhaps he will admire my shrewdness in pretending to have an errand, so as not to have him sit and talk to me. I will turn in and see the young Sculptor a moment, and then hurry back to finish the shoes for that brilliant fellow of Noyon."

Such were some of Berthelot's whispers as he dodged away from Friar Bernard, who was intent upon winning young men to the church of St. Saviour, in July, 1529. The friar was earnest, gentlemanly, and social. If Berthelot had sat on his bench and listened to the good man, he would not have found him a troublesome visitor. And if the monk had found that the young shoemaker could keep a secret, he would have told him something about the Bible and Luther's books, which the Milon family had never known.

Berthelot went into the statuary shop, where he heard the chisel of Vallette clicking upon the marble in the next room. Passing by a beautiful statue of the Virgin Mary, without bowing to it, he said, "How goes on the work?"

"Oh I am discouraged; I can never copy that model made by Michael Angelo. I find myself adoring it, and the chisel drops from my hand. I have had it set in the other room, that I may not see it so much, and then I may be less disgusted with my mean efforts."

"Absurd modesty! Angelo may come along one of these days and give you a better opinion of your own genius. But if your image were as little like the original as a post, it would be good enough for the purpose intended."

"What! do you call it an *image?*"

"Certainly I do. What else is it? It is a piece of idolatry, meant to catch eyes and hearts of superstitious people, who will bow to it and worship it, or do worse and make a goddess of Mary. I do not lift my hat to the exquisite model."

"My friend, I fear you have fallen into the heresy."

"Not at all; yet I know how the people, whose religion is that of the eye and the ear, the hands and the knees, will brand me. The Sorbonne is telling their spies, 'Keep watch for heretics. If any man does not lift his cap before an image, he is a heretic. If he hears the *Ave Maria* bell, and does not bow down, he is a heretic.' But mark you, a man may live as a rake and he is no heretic. This is what disgusts me with the hot-headed defenders of Popery."

Vallette tapped on the marble, and put a finger across his lips, in token of silence. A trowel was heard tingling on a new wall just by the door that opened into the marble-yard. The artist applied his chisel, and Berthelot his tongue, saying, "Your image will not get a bow from me, when it is set up in St. Saviour's, and if the priests don't like it they can burn me."

"Did you ever see a man burned?"

"Enough of men to please the most devout. I saw that good nobleman, Louis Berquin, last April, go up amid smoke and cloud from the front of Notre Dame, and the crime was horrible enough to have provoked an earthquake that would not have left one stone of the old Cathedral upon another. He was the most learned man of the nobility; he believed in freedom for himself and for all France. The tyrants tried to prove that he had a hand in mutilating the image of Mary, last year. There never was a more virtuous man. Let them go on, sparing us profligates, and hunting up the pious; let them arrest, condemn, quarter, crucify, burn, and behead; pirates can do this, and none but fiends will do it, but, if there be a just Judge over all, these persecutors must suffer."

Berthelot looked around after this outburst, for the trowel was silent, and there in the door, stood a bricklayer, with mouth agape, and eyes staring at the speaker. The poor man was astonished at hearing such words in that shop, and especially by the shoe-maker whom he had seen at work on his bench, as he passed that way. He could not have forgotten the fine countenance, and he took courage when he found himself partly recognized. Said he, "Do not fear me; I will not report you."

"I know you won't," replied Berthelot, "for you are a greater heretic than I am. Where did I see you going last night after dark?"

"I went to spend an hour with some friends."

"Aha! I know your friends. Fine thing for a bricklayer to be a friend of the merchant La Forge, and of Du Bourg, the draper! That's more than we shoemakers and sculptors are allowed to enjoy. I shall have to get me a trowel and a hod."

"It is not my poor trade that makes them my friends."

"No; and you would not dare tell your master what it is. Very pleasant little meetings you have there, I suppose. Perhaps you will let me come and sing for you. They are gospellers, I believe. Are you one?"

"Not any more of a gospeller than is the Lady Margaret, Queen of Navarre."

"So you put yourself on a level with the noble, brilliant, generous and pious queen! She is the grandest woman in France. She believes in liberty for you poor Christians, and would like to quench the fires on the Grêve with her tears. If it be a moral duty to reduce heretics to ashes, why don't these men, who thirst for Christian blood as they do for strong wine, swing her over a slow fire? She has more influence and leads more people to the Bible than all you harmless *Christaudins* put together. Let them burn down the tree, and you poor branches will wither by the heat. Beda should not draw such nice distinctions between the lofty and the lowly. He is very partial in his favours. Let him either strike all or spare all good Christians."

"May Heaven defend the noble queen, and save her from the stake!" exclaimed the bricklayer, who always heard fervent prayers for Margaret at the little meetings in the houses of La Forge, and other Christians of humbler life in the Latin quarter.

"Yes, you would rather burn yourself. I admire your choice. I wish Heaven might increase her power, for if she was in the place of her brother, King Francis, we would have none of our houses searched, nor any more Bible-readers led to the stake. But do you think she cares to notice you? I tell you, when you burn she won't be there. She could not save even the lordly Berquin. Don't imagine that when a poor bricklayer goes into the flames, you will attract much attention."

The humble man shuddered at the levity of these words and with the fear they excited, but with trembling lips and starting tears he said. "You may laugh at me, if you like, or try to frighten me, yet I do not trust in the friendships of this world. I have a friend greater than all the great."

"Pardon me; I was too rude. But please tell us what you think of the Virgin Mary. That is the test of everything in these days."

"I think she was an excellent woman, a good wife, a tender mother and a faithful disciple of her divine Son. I think she was a sinner by nature, and nothing but grace made her a saint. At least, so I read."

"In what?" The artist was startled to hear Mary called a sinner by nature; he was now standing with his eyes fixed upon the bricklayer, and trying to frown down what seemed to him a horrid blasphemy.

"Come now," continued Berthelot, "you have betrayed yourself. You mean the Testament. I dare say you have one hidden in the rubbish there. Some day your master will wonder why your trowel is not ringing, and he will slip through that door and catch you reading it; look out then for Beda. But trust me; I'll not turn informer. Now tell us where you go to church?"

"I go to St. Saviour's."

"Then you will have a chance to bow to this image one of these days, or burn for not bowing, unless Friar Bernard can save you. Do you know him?"

"He is my confessor—that is—when I have any."

"Then you can tell him that you keep company

with that young Noyon Student, who is so pale and thin, and whose light burns in his study later than even such rakes as I am walk the streets. I don't know his name, but he goes to your little meetings, and Friar Bernard will be there yet. But you must be at work. Conversation will be heresy before very long, and you must keep your tongue cold in secresy, and your neighbour must keep his chisel hot under the hammer. Be guarded against spies at your little gospel meetings, or you will soon cease to be Anthony Poille, of Meaux."

The bricklayer was amazed that Berthelot knew his name. The sculptor could not have told it, although for days they had been drinking from the same pitcher, and each had listened to the music of the other's toil.

"You knew the waterman," said Berthelot. "I saw you looking at him when he was burned. Had he any family?"

"A wife and two little children."

"Poor enough I'm sure. How do they live?"

"We help them as much as we can."

"I understand: you collect something for them at the little meetings. Your Testament somehow makes people very charitable. When did she see her husband for the last time?"

"On the morning of the day that he was seized. She waited long for him at dinner, but he never came."

"Was no visit granted her when he was in prison?"

"She was driven from the gate with a threat."

"I can imagine the rest. Take that and buy her a Testament." The bricklayer picked up a crown. "Take that and give her to buy whatever she wished her husband to purchase for the children." Three crowns lay on the floor. "Tell her to bring her children and see the man who sang for the martyred waterman while he was burning, and he will make each of them a pair of shoes."

"She will be very grateful——."

"Don't you let her send her thanks by you: I want her to come and bring them herself. I've a good reason for it. Now let us hear your trowel, or you may be turned off to starve."

Anthony went to his work, thinking that of all the mysterious beings he had ever met, this man was the strangest, and this was just the impression that Berthelot sought to produce. Thus he often appeared; now heartless, now all heart; at one moment asking in levity, "How would you like to be burned?" and the next draining his purse to bless an unknown widow and her little ones.

"Now you see if he does not lay up more bricks to-day than he did yesterday," said Berthelot to the Sculptor.

"Berthelot," said the artist, looking him in the face, "You might be as good a man as walks the St. Martin."

"Ho! don't I know that? You might as well tell me that I have black eyes and a Frenchman's face. Friar Bernard was broaching that delicate theme this morning, and I expect the Noyon student will give me the same hint when he finds that my revels have spoiled his shoes. I have heard him debating with Professor Cop on the law and the mass and holy relics, as they passed by our shop. One day they talked a long time at the door, and he kept telling the professor what "Paul says in Romans," and I should like to know if Paul did not write a book on law and against the pope."

"You must be far gone not to know who Paul was! He was a great Saint, next to St. Peter."

"That can't be the Paul they were speaking of, or else he is quite a different saint from any in your calendar. Why, I should suppose that the Noyon man considered him a fierce opposer of such a church as we see in our day."

"Did you never see his statue? Come here, for it is time that you knew something of him." They went into the front room, and stood before three fine statues. One was that of Mary, to which Berthelot had not bowed, and as Vallette looked devoutly at it he said "Ave Maria."

"Come now, let us have none of your devotions here," said Berthelot, who almost fancied the marble breathing a sigh of pity. "I admire it as a work of art, but I will not adore it as an idol."

"The statue on the left is that of St. Peter, the founder of our holy Church, with the keys in his hand."

"Ah! and you would have the keys used to lock up good Christians in prison until the weather is dry enough to make the green wood burn on the Grève. Don't tell me that St. Peter looks down and smiles upon the scene. I'll have to send the Noyon man here to tell you that St. Peter was never a pope, if he was even a bishop. I heard him say that much, for shoemakers are not deaf when doctors talk at their doors. But where is St. Paul?"

"There on the right: our grouping would be complete if the Virgin was seated on a throne as the queen of heaven, instead of standing as the Madonna, between the two apostles."

"And I imagine that if she were enthroned, Paul would take that sword, which he has, and drive her down from the royal seat, where the Lord alone should reign. But what is that book in his hand?"

"The Missal, I suppose."

"The Bible, I rather suspect, or else the great Law Book of the Romans, from which the young Noyonese took his best sayings. I'll inquire at the book-stalls for that old volume, and go to studying law. What if I should turn out to be a lawyer one of these years—the rival of young Viermey, the elegant horseman! Would it not be fine to have the Noyon Student sit by my bench and give me lectures, while I drove pegs in his boots!"

"I fear you are too much with the students already. They teach you to ridicule holy things."

"Better say that I teach them that art. I excel

them in it, for I was born with it in me, and they are a timid set, afraid of the priests, and in the leading strings of the doctors."

"But you seem to be a favourite among them."

"I make myself so. I ferret out a young man as soon as he comes into the Latin quarter, and show him the places of amusement. I make more shoes for them than the most devout catholic. But I detest them. They look down on me when they enter my shop, and order me about as their meanest servant. They will rise in the world, and we will be so low as to make their shoes for them. They will become great lawyers, and doctors, and fat bishops, and scarlet-capped cardinals, while we will remain poor hirelings—only you will be a great artist. I grow angry when I think I am nothing but a shoemaker's son, but I take my revenge on the students by leading them into the follies and profligacies of the city."

"Bad business; you are ruining yourself. I do not see why a shoemaker may not be as good as anybody. Just quit your free-thinking and your wild exploits, and if the Noyon student, whom you so much admire, can teach you anything to make you a sober man, listen to him. Only be guarded against heresy."

The artist returned to his work and plied his chisel again, for he had no time to lose. He felt somewhat more encouraged, after what his singular visitor had said, and he hoped that the poorer people might see some beauty in his statue when it should be placed near the confession-box of Friar Bernard. Perhaps they would, at least, understand whom it was meant to represent, and bow before it, not of course for its sake, but for the sake of the "glorious mother." A priest entered the door as Berthelot went out. Their eyes met and spoke a little volume of fire to each other, but they both were too haughty for the least nod of their proud heads. They had met when the waterman was burned, and as Berthelot was singing, the priest had struck him on the lips. The shoemaker had booked the account for a future settlement, when they should meet at one of Berthelot's masked balls.

Tielly, the priest, began to tell the Sculptor of the latest miracles performed by the broken image that had been removed from the St. Antoine quarter to the Church of St. Germain. A child that had not lived through its first day, in this world, was brought before the headless image; the colour of the little dead face changed to a live flush; the mother fancied that its hands grew warm, and its heart was beating; it was baptized and then died the second time! The poor woman was comforted in thinking that Mary had taken it to heaven. But Tielly had something more wonderful to relate, and he said, "A priest was preaching there last Sunday, and when describing the sorrows of the Virgin, he looked at the broken image and exclaimed, 'Hark! I hear the glorious Mother sighing over the treatment she receives.' The audience started up and saw the statue trembling."

"Did you see it?"

"No; and between you and me I doubt whether any one else did. It was a new sensation, planned beforehand. If the statue can work miracles, why don't it repair itself and appear some morning fully restored to its original perfection."

"What is to become of us when you priests turn infidels?" asked Vallette, and the reply was, "Trick the people out of their money and then spend it in a gay life as we do. Only dupes are serious in these days."

CHAPTER III.

THE LITTLE MEETINGS.

ON the way to his shop Berthelot fell in with a bird of his own feather. It was Robert Daniel, a young brother of the celebrated lawyer, Francis Daniel at Orleans. He had come to Paris to see the world, and the shoe-maker was able to lead him into some of its darkest corners. As they had not met for some time, they had much to relate, and having told of a few late frays, Berthelot inquired, "Has your sister really taken the veil?"

"Yes, and the giddy creature will find that she has made a great mistake. She loves the world as much as I do, but her teachers made her believe that it was a very romantic thing to bury herself in a nunnery."

"She would have found much more romance in our lively circles. It grieves me to think that I shall never dance with her again, unless I break into the convent some night and bring her out into freedom. Why did not her friends reason with her?"

"That is all the trouble. They reasoned in the wrong way. They persuaded her to be a nun. Even my brother, the advocate, did not oppose it, if she would only take the veil willingly and not by constraint."

"What could have possessed them?"

"I can tell you. It was their fear that she would become a heretic. She was an ardent admirer of the Queen of Navarre, and they began to write letters to each other. The queen sent her a Testament and some of her religious poems. My sister could not keep from showing them, and then her teachers began with their crafty arts."

"Just tell me when you learn that she is tired of her gloomy cage, and I will find a way to let the bird go free," said Berthelot on reaching the door of his shop. Robert would have gone on, but a glance showed him that the older Milon was out and young Coiffard was in, waiting for just such a meeting as these three bosom friends desired.

"Well, Berthelot, if you would give less time to balls and more to your bench, you would earn better wages. You will not have my slippers done in time for our next grand dance."

"Robert, please reduce this fellow's wrath, and then I will talk to him," said Berthelot, as he prepared himself for work. He sat down on his bench, took up a shoe that was nearly finished, and applied himself to it until the toil bedewed his brows. His visitors watched him and foolishly thought that it was a disgrace for so fine a looking young man to be the poor servant of a shoe-hammer.

"For what student are you making those?"

asked Coiffard. "I see they are in the university style."

"I don't know his name," replied Berthelot, rapping away in earnest. "He was once here under Master Mathurin Cordier, and afterwards was in Montaigu College, but he was so timid and studious that I thought him out of my reach. He is now here again; a short, slender, pale, serious-looking man of about twenty, who walks with Professor Cop and talks like a learned doctor. As Cop's father is physician to the King, I dare say this Noyon man will be high chancellor before many years—if he is not too great a heretic."

"I know him," said the two visitors both at once.

"And you like him too, I fancy. He is as neat in his dress as a prince, and as precise in his talk as if he had studied logic all his life," said Berthelot. "He can tell a man just how he wants his work made, and in as elegant language as if he were delivering the farewell of his class to the faculty."

"He was born to be a scholar," added Coiffard, who was crowding in his praises. "Why, up at Noyon, they made him a chaplain when twelve years old, shaved his head and gave him a small benefice. Two years ago they gave him a parish, but he is too much of a scholar ever to be a priest. Last year he studied law at Orleans, and was so learned that the professors used to invite him to lecture in their place. I heard him, and he was brilliant. I often met him, Robert, at the house of your brother.

"He is the man who went with Professor Cop to the nunnery to learn whether my sister was perfectly willing to take the veil," said Robert. "It was my brother's request, and if she had not been so deluded she would have escaped with him. But she spoke of her vows, with as much levity, as if she were playing with her doll. If Francis had trusted me with his errand, I would have brought her away, however the nuns might have howled."

"Why don't you tell us his name?" asked Berthelot.

"It is John Calvin. Orleans will long have anecdotes to tell about him," added Coiffard. "One day, after a lecture by the great star of the law, (Pierrel'Etoile,) he walked up and down the hall with the other students who were glad to see him becoming less bashful and more familiar. Pulling out his knife, he went up to a pillar, and carved a C, then an A, then an L, and so on until the word CALVIN stood out boldly for priests to scoff at in future time, because he will be a dreadful heretic if he escapes Beda and his detectives."

"A first-rate heretic already," said Berthelot, "for I have seen him going to La Forge's little meetings."

"Those little meetings are no new thing," Robert hastened to say. "Calvin began them at Orleans. He tried to persuade me into them, but it was too serious a business for my taste. He would have changed all my fine plans for pleasure. The fact is

4

nobody can withstand him when he has the Bible in his hand."

"He did not put himself forward," said Coiffard. "The students and towns-people begged him to come and teach them. He was abashed. He tried to hide away in the libraries or along the banks of the river. But they followed him, and he was compelled to say, 'All my hiding-places are turned into schools.' Then the citizens urged him into their houses, where he explained the Scriptures. He afterwards went to Bourges and taught in private houses, and in the neighbouring castles and villages."

"He is the man for me," said Berthelot. "When I conclude to become sober I must send for him."

"Send for him! You assume a vast importance," said Robert, with a boisterous laugh.

"I'll go to the little meetings, then, and hear him."

"You did not know how near I came to having him for a companion," said Coiffard. "My father thought it would be a fine plan to keep me out of such wild company as the present."

"A very desirable thing, if you had the good sense to perceive it," remarked Berthelot, rather dryly.

"I happened to see him at the inn the day he arrived, a few weeks since. My father and I went to invite him to take lodgings at our house. Of course, I entreated him, and I never knew father beg so hard for a guest. But he was not to be persuaded."

"He knew you too well," Berthelot rejoined, holding up the shoe that he had finished, as a specimen of his best skill. "He didn't wish the job of taming such a fractious colt."

"He wanted to lodge nearer the school, where he could attend Professor Danés' Greek course. So I was not caught in that net, and was left free to choose you profligates for my genial companions."

"I am glad you appreciate us," said Berthelot, "and we must try to hold you under good influences. You will go with us to one of the gospel meetings, I suppose?"

"Certainly; name the time."

"To-night; I'll find out the place. Be here early. But remember that there must be no unfair play, no spying, no informing. If we should be tortured by Beda, there must not be one word extorted from us against those harmless people. I do not want to believe as they do, but I'd rather be broken on the wheel than inform on one poor man who would be certain to go to the flames."

"I don't propose to go," said Robert, who was cautious of meeting Calvin, for he suspected that his brother had urged him to seek this lost sheep and send him back to Orleans. After some debate, and the pledge of his two friends that they would certainly be at the coming ball, he consented to the plan.

At the sign of the *Pelican* in the rue de St. Martin, lived the merchant La Forge. He was one who could be diligent in business and fervent in spirit, serving the Lord. Noble, tender-hearted, and generous, his neighbours wondered whether he would not share all that he had with the poor, and at length come to poverty. "I am thankful," he would say, "for all the blessings that God has bestowed upon me, and I will not be sparing of my wealth, either to comfort the needy or to spread the glorious gospel." He printed the Scriptures at his own expense, and gave copies along with his liberal alms. The poor all had a refuge at the *Pelican.*

"We will be glad to see you at our house to-night," he would say to the lowly disciples who made their little purchases; "but it is not my feast, it is the great supper of the King, to which I invite you."

"But I have no better shoes than these," or "this is the only coat I've got," they would say, "and I am not worthy to enter under your roof."

"Jesus says, 'Come unto me.' The Spirit and the bride say, Come. Let him that heareth say, Come, and take of the water of life freely. The King will say, Bring forth the best robe and put it on him, and put shoes on his feet."

In this way the little meetings were appointed. At one meeting there was no notice of the time or place of the next, lest the officers might send their spies or their soldiers to the spot. Privately the word was whispered about, or a scarlet thread was carelessly yet carefully dropped at the door, caught on a post, or hung out of a window, as from the house of Rahab in the olden time. This thread had told Berthelot of the intended meeting at La Forge's, but the whole Inquisition could not have made him reveal the secret. The prudent wife had everything in readiness so that even the prying busy-body, who had called, and who put herself in the way of an invitation to supper, did not suspect what was going on.

"How shall we get rid of her?" whispered the good wife to her husband, when it began to grow dark. "It will not do to have her here at the meeting, she is such a gossip."

"Let me manage it," he replied. So, entering the room, he said to her, "You were telling us of a poor woman, whom you feared had nothing to eat. I want to send something to her, and as every hour may seem very long to her, I, perhaps, should send my errand-boy at once. Can you tell the house?"

"No, let me carry it. Of course I did not expect you to do what her nearest neighbours should be doing. It is very kind in you, and what we do we must do quickly. Certainly I'll carry it. I am always glad to give alms"—especially when others furnish them, she might have added. She went with quite a variety of charities, and very likely presented them as her own gifts. Thus the way was clear. One by one the people began to assemble.

At precisely the right moment, a young man left his room in the college of Fortret; passed two or three doors in the Latin quarter, where he saw the scarlet thread somewhere in front of the houses; stepped briskly over the island, and, as he glanced at the towers of Notre-Dame, felt like going to the spot and pouring forth his grief over the burning of Berquin; and went northward up the street of St. Martin, until he came to the crossing of the great boulevard that reaches from the church of the Madeleine. He had met the bricklayer in the best suit that he could afford; there was little chance to talk, for the people were crowding down from St. Dennis', and there might be spies among them. "I'll soon be there," said Anthony Poille, and they parted.

The student saw that the street was not clear at the sign of the *Pelican*, and made a little circuit through other streets, nervously calling up again the points on which he would speak at the meeting. He saw others strolling as he was, knew them and their purpose, but scarcely greeted them. Coming round to the Pelican, he entered the house of La Forge, and was warmly saluted as John Calvin.

"This way for a moment," said the merchant, leading him into a side room. "We must be cautious to-night. I sent a man to St. Dennis' this evening, and he heard a priest exciting the hearers against us, and quite nearly pointing out our meeting-places. We must change the signal."

"Let it be a green straw with a knot tied in it, and left in some nook about the door, or an egg broken on the pavement, or, where there is a little yard in front, let three roses or lilies be partly broken, so as to hang drooping. Let all these be employed."

"Just the thing; I will whisper the signs to the faithful. Delay a while; the people are wary and late, and please be short." La Forge was busy sending the chairs and benches from the parlours to the remotest rooms of the house, for on a sudden the place had been changed. Persons of almost every calling and condition entered through different doors. At length all intending to come were supposed to be present, except the bricklayer.

"I will read the psalm, but it must not be sung to-night," said Calvin, as he began the services. The exercises were those of a simple social prayer-meeting. One or two men drew forth refreshing words from the hidden depths of their own experience to comfort those who were tempted or tried, in fear or affliction. But all were looking for the rising of "the young expounder" as they called him.

Calvin rose, modestly, timidly, and with a trembling of the hand that held his Bible. He looked like one who had been fasting in order to feast on the riches of learning. His eye was a bright lamp when turned upon the Scripture page. Not many months before, that Bible was unknown by him;

now, every leaf bore marks of study, if not of tears. He glanced at his hearers, who filled every space that he could see. It was the largest meeting he had attended. There sat or stood poor women, who had toiled all day long for bread; servants, who had waited, unsuspected, at tables where fierce persecutors had dined and vented their threats over their wine; coachmen, who had thrown off the livery worn when they drove their masters to parliament to sit on the trial of a man that would never be at these meetings again; labourers, whose hands were roughened by the hammer, the trowel, and the spade; salesmen, who covertly sold a Testament to a known customer; students, who once had come to scoff, but now came to pray, with a few tutors from the colleges; physicians, whose dying patients had first taught them the gospel, and two or three men somewhat learned in the law. The noble face of Surgeon Pointet was seen farthest back in the hall, reminding Calvin of Luke, the beloved physician.

The text was read—"Fear not, little flock; for it is your Father's good pleasure to give you the kingdom." It went like a reviving cordial to many a wounded and fearful heart. "It is the Good Shepherd, who says this," remarked Calvin, as he entered upon a description of "the great Shepherd of the sheep." A slight noise was heard; the faces of three men were seen near Surgeon Pointet, and Calvin hesitated. All eyes were turned, and some could see the shoemaker, whose face they admired, but whose hand they feared, and his two scoffing associates. La Forge was not a little confused. Berthelot saw that he was not quite welcome, and whispered, "I pledge you that we have come with no ill intent, and that we are under an oath of secrecy."

The Surgeon nodded to Calvin, and to increase his assurance, the short quiet bricklayer contrived to make his face visible, by stretching up on tip-toe, and his smile was a telegram, saying, "I brought them here." Berthelot felt humbled in his own estimation, by the suspicion he had drawn on himself, and quite sorry that he had excited so much fear. The three young men would have left, but the silence was only for a moment.

"Yes, the Good Shepherd tells you, Fear not little flock," Calvin resumed. "Not yet do we find grievous wolves entering among us to devour, but if we did, the Shepherd can save. He is the Saviour." The Saviour was represented, seeking the lost, gathering his flock, and laying down his life for the sheep. Berthelot was glad to know that he was not pointed out as a wolf, and before the true cross he may have stood beholding, wondering, and ready to exclaim with the Centurion, "Verily, this was the Son of God!"

"Although there are no wolves among you, yet do you all belong to the little flock of Christ?" was Calvin's close question to his hearers; and Berthelot felt the speaker's burning eye, as he told them how to decide the question, and proved to them that this flock was the true Church, that the "gates of hell should not prevail against it;" that deadly persecution only sent the true sheep to the great fold in heaven, and that faith in Jesus was victor over every fear. "Enough that you have such a Shepherd and such a fold," said he, "but you have more. You have a Father and a Father's house. You have a Kingdom, and therefore a King. You have your Father's good pleasure towards you and in you. If it be his good pleasure that we suffer with Jesus, we shall also reign with him. The martyrs are reigning with him now. Your homes may be desolate, but heaven is being peopled. Your tears may fall, but they are singing the song of the redeemed. You are bereaved, but they are glorified."

One poor woman drew Berthelot's attention. He suspected that she was the widow of the martyred waterman. Her head was bowed down with the burden of her awful memories, until she heard of the victory, and the reign, and the glory of the martyrs; then turning her face heavenward and folding her hands, she seemed as a breathing statue of resignation. Berthelot would never forget that countenance. The lively, active, intelligent Coiffard was also deeply moved by what he saw and heard. If any heart was not yet touched, it must have been thrilled as Calvin ended with the passage in which are the words, "If God be for us, who can be against us?"

After a fervent prayer, especially for "those who were yet reserved for the trial by fire and the victory by death," a notice was given that the families of several martyrs were in need of help, and that they should not be forgotten during the next week.

"Pass around your hat," said Berthelot to the bricklayer, loudly enough for almost all to hear. Anthony hesitated. "If you don't I will." The bricklayer saw that Surgeon Pointet approved, and others began to extend their hands. Berthelot contributed as if he had forgotten what he had given in the morning, and left himself nothing to squander, had he been inclined to spend his midnight in a tavern.

Through different doors the people left the house. The three young men were in the advance, and began to tell what they thought of the services, when they met a man who was prowling about to make his discoveries. Berthelot stopped; looking the man in the face he asked, "Do you know that I am no heretic?"

"Certainly I do. Don't I meet you at the balls?"

"Then cease your spying in these quarters. Cannot I and my friends have a social evening in any way we think best, without your eye being upon us? March home and tell your master that Berthelot Milon and his friends have spent an hour in a very pleasant way, and let them make the most of it."

"If I may judge the whole company by the specimens now before me, there is nothing to concern Beda. Good night."

"No, you are not off in that direction. Come with us." The spy joined them, and on the way they said not a word about the sermon. The report to Beda's agent was, "It was only a short meeting of Berthelot and his friends." The Christians would not have justified this prevarication. Instead of the scarlet thread at the sign of the Pelican, the Christians must look for the knotted straw at the sign of the Black Horse.

CHAPTER IV.

CRIPPLED FOR LIFE.

AMUSEMENT has often been fatal to religious convictions. Whatever good impressions Berthelot and his associates received at the place of prayer, were lost in the house of mirth. We can imagine how they talked by day and caroused at night. Calvin had given them up as almost hopeless, and for months had seen little of them.

"Well, what do you think," said Robert, one day in January, as he entered the shoe-shop. "Your model of excellence has invited me to dine with him to-morrow, and to hide the trap he has asked me to bring Coiffard along. Don't you feel slighted?"

"Not in the least. Calvin would look well having his cobbler to dine with him. You two gentlemen have been well educated—or as well as you were willing to be. The air was full of learning and you had only to breathe it. If you do not have anything to say, you ought to be so accomplished as to keep silent and enjoy his conversation."

"I do not propose to enjoy it. He wishes to read me a lecture on self-destruction."

"Which might be very useful to you."

"I suspect my half-heretic brother has been setting him upon me. Not long ago he took a long walk with me to renew his persuasions. He said that if I would not enter on a new course of study, I ought to return to Orleans. I told him it was utterly vain to urge that advice, and finally cut him so short that he was silenced. I thought that I had conquered him. He would part with me, however, as if nothing had injured his feelings."

"His calmness was his victory. He knows that such volcanoes as you are may be managed best by letting them take their own time to cool. When the lava had lost its heat, I suppose he trampled over it and approached you again."

"No more strong figures of speech, if you please. Yesterday he very politely hinted that we should have a fair talk on the subject, and he asked me to come and dine with him. It would give him great pleasure; he meant that it would afford me great profit."

"You will go, of course."

"Perhaps, if I do not go somewhere else." Robert then told of certain other plans that he had suddenly formed.

The next day Calvin had a tempting dinner prepared, for, having done all he could to win the wild youth, he now hoped to succeed in persuading him to return home. The hour came, but no guests. He waited and still waited. Then he sent a messenger to Robert's lodgings. "He has decamped," said the landlord. "He has left for Italy." Calvin was grieved, and discouraged in the attempt to gain this class of young men. To throw off his sadness, he, shortly after, took the winter air, and made an exploring visit through the Latin quarter, and explained the Bible to those, who met under the shadow of the night in remote houses to worship God. "The word of Christ is always a fire," they said, "but when he explains it, the fire shines out with unusual brilliancy." This part of the city was afterwards called *Little Geneva.*

Three days before Good Friday, came the procession of the Fat Ox. The same thing had occurred on a Sunday before Lent, but Berthelot was then lying on a pile of leather, in sickening disgust from his excesses during the Carnival. His purse was now empty and he was at work on his bench. He heard the music and dropped his awl. A train of butchers, dressed in fantastic styles, came marching down the St. Martin as the body guard of a fat beef. The ox was covered with embroidery and laurel, and on him sat a child, called "king of the butchers," decorated with a blue scarf, and holding in one hand a sword and in the other a sceptre. Berthelot saw it all and summed up his opinion in one strong word—"Nonsense!"

He cared nothing for Lent, and his social companions joined with him in his special efforts to keep up their midnight revels during that season. It is against my conscience to take any of my readers to a ball; we will only go to an ancient door that once shut a certain stairway from the street in the Latin quarter. The time was five o'clock on a morning long ago. The dancing and drinking, and what was even worse, had been going on all night, among the maskers. At the head of the stairs a fray had occurred. A tall, stately and free young man, whom everybody knew by his graceful bearing, had been narrowly watching an over-fed rough monk, who had crept in under a mask, and for all that he was quite as well known. The one was admired, the other despised by the godless company. The monk had taken pains to treat the dancers' favourite with rudeness, whenever they met. At last he felt a pull, his mask was snatched away, and a voice shouted, "You are the monk that struck my face on the Gréve, when the waterman was burned. You warned the sculptor, Vallette, not to allow me his friendship. But these are nothing. You take the money of the poor, at the confession-box, and spend it in these revels. You pretend to teach us reckless youths the beauty and glory of religion. Come, show us your bloated face, and tell us how to be devout. Prove to us that your religion consists in burning heretics and in playing the debauchee!"

The monk could say nothing. yet his anger consumed his shame. He was burly enough to hold his own in a fight, and he flung himself against his accuser. They whirled each other about, and finally went rolling down the stairs. An awful wail was heard rising up from the pavement. The party came rushing down in excitement. The monk had fled. A crowded circle bent over the groaning man, saying, "Poor, poor Berthelot!"

What priest? What surgeon? were the questions that perplexed even the students who were present. It seemed as if dozens of messengers were speeding for dozens of confessors and physicians, and yet really nobody was running upon such an errand. A score of houses were proposed where he might be taken, but there was no truly good Samaritan in all the crowd whose sinful mirth had been so suddenly changed to improvident mourning.

"We must take him home," said Coiffard. He got his large coat, turned it into a sort of hammock, by having a man hold each of the four corners, had Berthelot laid in it, and led the bearers to the river bank. It was then clear daylight. A frail, sorrowful woman was unlocking the chain of her little boat, and it seemed the only one that would be ready for half an hour. They were stepping into it, when a scream of agony led one of them to say, "Poor Berthelot! we can't help it. We will be as careful as possible." He knew not one word that was said. But the woman was surprised at that name. It was engraven on her memory.

"Let me get some pillows," said she, dropping her oar.

"It will take too long. The man will die before

we get him home," replied Coiffard, whose selfishness had prevented the growth of sympathy.

"It is only a few steps to my house," she answered, having already begun her race. Soon Berthelot was pillowed softly in the boat; two men were at the oars, and the woman was gazing on the attractive face of the sufferer. He threw one hand over into the water, and feeling its pleasant coolness he smiled. She bathed the other hand; then moistened his temples and his whole face. His eyes resumed their naturalness, and were fixed on the kind woman. There was joy in the little boat when he said, "This is delightful rowing. How came I here? Ah! don't tell me, I know it all."

"I am so glad that I came out this morning earlier than usual," said the voice of the tender woman. "My children are well again, and I can earn something now."

"Are you not a *Christaudine?*" whispered Berthelot. She glanced at the company, and this was answer enough. She was not sure that she had rightly guessed at the man. There might be a score of Berthelots, and she did not think that her benefactor would keep such company as had gathered on the bank to see him in the boat.

"Slow, friends," said Berthelot, "row slowly; let us enjoy the fresh air." They however persuaded him that the dampness might injure him, and were soon at the landing.

"Why have you not come to have those shoes

made?" said Berthelot to the woman, and she then fully knew who he was. "I may never make any more shoes, but if I take one of your soft pillows home under my aching head, will you come after it?" His wits had evidently returned; he had a scheme in his quick mind.

"Certainly, or if I do not, you are welcome to it," she replied.

"Pay her double fare," was Berthelot's order, most willingly fulfilled on the part of his companions, for the stingy Coiffard knew that none of it would come from his purse.

"Your husband," whispered Berthelot, while the others were preparing to carry him, "was a martyr on the Gréve; I sang for him when he was gaining his last victory: now I shall, perhaps, be a martyr to my own follies and sins, and you must come and cheer me in my righteous punishment."

"I do thank you for your kindnesses to me. It was only your money that kept my boat from being sold," said the wife of the martyred waterman, in broken words and with falling tears. "May God bless you"——. The helpless man was borne away in pain to his home, but the woman's sighs went sounding in his ears, and grew softer as they mingled with his memories of her devotion at La Forge's, and her gentleness in the boat, until they were to him like the lingering music of a holy psalm.

What of Berthelot during the restless days and sleepless nights of his agony? Surgeon Pointet exerted all his skill, doubting whether it were possible for the patient to recover. Friar Bernard was absent, or he would have been called to afford instruction and comfort. In his stead was a priest who held the rites of the Romish Church as altogether essential to salvation; a man who adored the so-called Virgin Mary, and saw more virtue in a crucifix than in the true cross of the crucified Saviour. The church, and not the Christ, was the word ever on his lips.

"Oh if you could only be carried to St. Germain and laid before the broken statue of the glorious mother," said this priest, "you might be healed!"

"Nonsense!" was Berthelot's reply. The subject was dropped. The confessor must try new arts and more gentleness. He changed his tactics. He even pretended to love the liberty of thought that Berthelot had asserted, and to be utterly opposed to the burning of Christians. "True they are heretics," said he, "but they have a right to life so long as God spares them." He pretended to approve of the reading of the Bible, but yet was careful never to read it to the sufferer.

Berthelot was not the man to be caught with guile. He simply endured the priest very much as he endured the physician. Pointet could not induce him to apply the remedies prescribed, and still he had some happiness in seeing the surgeon coming every day and often spending an hour in conversation. But all talk upon the gospel seemed in vain.

"I detest the priests for burning innocent people," he would say, "yet I will not be a Lutheran." (This was the term applied to those who adhered to the Bible and forsook the Roman church.) Then at another time, when the priest was with him, he would say, "I detest the new doctrines of these gospellers, yet I abominate the lives of you priests."

All at once the surgeon stopped his visits. Berthelot missed him, for as he had been allowed only two visitors, he liked Pointet far more than the priest. "What is the use of his coming if you will not take his remedies?" said his mother, whose devotion to her pitiable son was untiring; "he has taken some offence, but if you need a physician we will send for Doctor Laval."

"I understand the offence," said Berthelot. "The priest has interfered. He has alarmed you, lest the good surgeon should teach me to believe as he does. My father must deal honestly with me if he expects to win me back to the religion that filled me with zeal in my childhood."

"My dear son, we would give everything if you would become again as devout"——

"And as superstitious?"

"Please do not talk so. It was a comfort in those days to see you cross yourself so gracefully, and sprinkle yourself with the holy water at the church door, and bow to the saints, and hear your sweet voice say the *Ave Maria*, and answer your many, many questions about the mass and the stations. Do not call it superstition. It is our blessed religion."

"If there is any true religion, it is far more than all that."

"Surely it is; and if we are faithful to the church, God will give us a great deal of merit for doing what you think is of no account. Just think how you have fallen from the faith of your fathers! And now you are punished for saying such hard things against the church and the priests and the glorious mother."

"Perhaps I am, but I know of greater sins than those, and it is much more likely that I am suffering from them. Do not weep. Let us talk of something more pleasant. Has that kind woman called to get her pillow?"

"Yes, and we told her that no one could see you until you were better."

"That is all that she came for—to see me. Why did you not let me know of her call? I know when it was. The priest was here at the time, and he interfered. Is he to rule over this house?" Berthelot had hit upon the truth. It must not be pressed. The priest was again heard in the shop, just beyond a thin partition.

"Has he asked you again to send for that heretic?" inquired the priest, of Milon the father.

"Yes, he constantly urges it. He devises all sorts of plans to get word to him. I think we must yield a little in the case."

"Not one inch. Once introduce that man here, and he will sit with that Lutheran Bible in his hand and terrify your son into the most accursed doctrines. Better let him remain the veriest rake on earth"——.

"What is that you say?" cried Berthelot, and the priest entered the next room as bland and gentle as a lamb, or rather a fox. "I know of whom you speak—young Calvin."

"I would not have you think so for one moment," the deceitful priest answered. "Surely if it would do you any good to see Calvin, you should be gratified."

"Then send for him."

"Of course we will, when the right time comes, and when your mind is more calm, and when your wise judgment has fully regained its former vigour." It was only by force that Berthelot restrained his tongue from exposing this hypocrisy and injustice. As such tricks were daily brought to his notice, he was becoming used to them.

Weeks wore slowly away, and Berthelot's injuries grew worse. He had the use of scarcely any of his members except his arms and his tongue. All the rest "died little by little," as Crispin tells in his *Martyrs*. And he became a helpless paralytic for life. He, who had once been so proud of his beauty, so admired as a favourite, so bold in his exploits, and so eager for mirth, was now weak, broken-down, unable to associate with his gay companions, and denied a sight of those for whose visits he pined. He grew more morose, crisp, and sarcastic than ever.

"Do carry me into the shop, and let me lie where I can see the people passing," he entreated his parents. The ruling priest opposed it, because he might draw in some of the heretics to see him. But his parents saw how the lion fretted in his cage, and at last consented. Every day he was carried into the shop. It required four men to remove him, and only then with great pain to himself. It once delighted him to be stared at in admiration; now it irritated him to have a glance from strangers, for their eyes were drawn upon his deformity. "What a misfortune!" many said to his father in the shop.

"It was not always so," the old man answered, partly because of his former pride in his son, and partly because he might prevent him from breaking out in an angry retort. "Not always so; he was quite another person in his youth, and you would have been charmed with his excellent gifts."

One day he was propped up near the window, when he saw the wife of the martyred waterman passing. Their eyes met and they greeted each other at the same instant. "Come in," said he. "Father, please show this good friend a seat. It was she who fixed the pillows for me."

The youth of the old shoemaker seemed to be renewed. Never was his strap flung more quickly from his knee, and a chair put forward. That would not do—he must see her in a better one, and his loose slippers went shuffling into the next room for the best chair in the house. With reluctance she took it, and there he stood, arranged his glasses, gazed at the poor, blushing boat-woman and said, "If it had not been for you, my son Bartholomew would not have been alive to-day. He has talked every day about you, and I was going to the river to ask you to come and see him some day, but I feared you would be losing time and money by such a favour."

She replied to this speech as best she could, and then the mother came to pour upon her the warm gratitude of her soul. She was utterly confused, but Berthelot began to manage the interview. It is natural for a widow to delight in telling the story of her good husband's deeds and death, and he touched this ever-tuned chord of her heart. She told it all, and unconsciously divulged the fact that she and her husband once had known prosperous days at Meaux, where they had a comfortable home, a thriving business, books, friends and happiness. It was their social influence that made them a mark for the terrible agents of Beda, who drove them forth in the night, each carrying a little child, and leaving all else to fall into the hands of the cruel hunters of heresy.

"Is there no law by which you can regain your property?" inquired Berthelot. "I wish I had been a lawyer."

"Poor people can get nothing by law," said she, "but I am often told by the priests that if I will renounce my religion and become a penitent in the Church, the property will all be restored."

"Surely it would," said the credulous Madame Milon, who believed that such tempting offers were made in good faith.

"Why don't you do it?" asked the elder Milon.

The woman was abashed at finding that she was not among Bible Christians, although she knew Berthelot's opinions. But faith is courageous. She had committed herself, and there was no retreat, and without much hesitation she replied,

"I would not do it for the world. Even if I got back my home, I would live in it as a wretched traitor to my Lord. I am not so poor as he was, nor so persecuted. I am happy and contented, for I hope that I have some of the riches of Christ. I could lose my husband—but oh! it was horrible to see him burned—yet he is glorified."

The elder Milons had never heard the like, and they were secretly lamenting that heresy could so delude a poor artless woman. In their eyes she was possessed with an evil spirit.

The sobbing visiter looked at the mother, saying, "It was a great comfort to him and to me, in that awful hour, to have your son sing as he did on the Gréve."

This was news to Berthelot's parents, and they stared at everything in their astonishment, but a second thought brought up the fact that no exploit had been too strange or daring for him to attempt. "And what would I have done for a Testament," she added, "if he had not sent me one."

Another item of astounding news. They asked Berthelot to explain, which he did to their silence, if not to their satisfaction. There had been days when the least hint of such favour to the Bible-readers would have put the poor woman into the street. They would have vented the wrath they felt against their son, upon the object of his kindness. But could they be angry at him, crippled as he was? could they ill-treat one to whom, the Surgeon Pointet said, they owed Berthelot's life? They sought relief by changing the subject, and asking about her children, her house, and her earnings.

"Now," said Berthelot, "you did not favour me by coming for those shoes. Father, please hand me down that box. I made some once that I hoped might suit. They will be the better for seasoning."

The woman—whose name was found to be Maria Jardinet—protested, but at length, under the urgent persuasion of the three Milons, consented to put her feet into a finer pair than she had worn since her weary wandering from her home at Meaux, and to carry with her some gaily trimmed pairs for her little ones. Berthelot had passed the happiest hour of his helplessness, and his mother had a reason for saying to the visitor at parting, "Come often and see us."

CHAPTER V.

THE WONDER OF PARIS.

The marriage of King Francis and Eleanor brought a merry day to Paris. The less happiness there was in this political union, the more pomp was desired by the monarch. Clement Marot wrote,

"There were mysteries and games, and the streets were gaily drest
And the roads were strewn with flowers, the sweetest and the best;
On every side were galleries, and, if 'twould pleasure yield,
We'd have conjured up again for thee a new Elysian field."

Berthelot saw part of these gayeties, and he grew still more restive and unhappy. He was angry because his former habits were denied him for ever, and he must vent his spite on somebody. He jeered at the smiling crowds, and freely poured forth his sarcasms.

"Halloa! you Lutheran!" he one day shouted to a quiet Christian whose eye of compassion was turned upon him as he was passing. "Why don't you stop and stare at a miserable wretch? Keep your pity for yourself; you will be burned one of these days."

The Christian came up to the window, was touched

at the sight, and said affectionately, "Poor man, why do you mock at us? Do you not see that *God has bent your body in this way, in order to straighten your soul?*"

A new thought entered the mind of the paralytic. "Can it be," he asked himself, "that God has made me helpless so that he might reform me?"

"Pardon me for speaking so abruptly," the stranger went on to say, when he saw that his arrow had gone to the heart of the reviler. "I surely would not injure your feelings."

"You are right; my soul is bent; it has met with a fearful fall some time."

"It fell in Adam, and has been falling ever since, and now it's very crooked and helpless, or you would not mock at us. But it may be raised and fully restored by our Lord Jesus, 'who, when he was reviled, reviled not again,' and 'who his own self bare our sins in his own body on the tree, that we, being dead to sin should live unto righteousness. For ye were as sheep going astray; but are now returned unto the Shepherd and Bishop of your souls.'"

Berthelot had been astonished many times, because these humble disciples would bear his insults, and yet make no reply, but now he felt subdued by the gentle tone of the stranger, who, at length, gave him a New Testament, saying, "Look at this book, and a few days hence you will tell me what you think of it."

When Berthelot was left alone, he said to himself

"So this book that I hated, and would not read lest it should put a check on my bad habits, and convince me that I must repent, has, at last, come into my hands. I'll see what it is makes the Christians so kind, so patient under derision, so forgiving and so courageous."

He opened it, he began to taste a new fruit, he could not put aside such a wondrous book, and he read it day and night. It became his teacher; he needed no other. The sword of the Spirit cut the way to his heart, and the Lord took the strong-hold. His past life began to terrify him. His cry was "Oh, my sins, my sins, they haunt me like wolves. I cannot flee from them."

"Send for Friar Bernard," said his mother, one day when she overheard him crying, for mercy. "He is now in the city again."

"No; this book does not tell me to send for priests, but to go to Jesus. If he would only say to me, as he did to the man sick of the palsy, and helpless as I am, 'Son, thy sins are forgiven thee!' I would not ask him also to say, 'Arise, take up thy bed and walk.'"

"But, my son, you cannot go to see Jesus."

"I do not need to see him. Oh, if I could only believe in him!"

This was his chief thought and wish for days and weeks together. Persons would pass by his window and notice that he was absorbed in his Testament, or if they came into the shop, he did not seem to notice them unless they were familiar friends. He did not even see Friar Bernard as he walked slowly past, until, one day, their eyes met. The friar saw that he was welcome, and came in, took the poor sufferer by the hand, and as they talked they wept together.

"These sins, so black and fierce!" said Berthelot. "If I could only believe, I am sure Jesus would take them away."

"Does the crucifix help you any?"

"Not at all. Please do not mention the little crosses nor images. I want the true cross."

"I am glad to hear you say so. Why do you not pray, 'Lord, I believe; help thou my unbelief?'"

Silently, and with eyes turned to heaven, the paralytic was lying, all absorbed in thought or prayer. At last he said, "Yes, yes, my unbelief—I understand that. I have not been willing to believe, nor even to learn the truth. I have insulted you when you have been trying to teach me. Can you forgive me?"

"I cherish nothing against you that is not already pardoned."

"Then you freely overlook all my offences. How kind, how full of love you are to a poor wretch!"

"Why should I not be? The blessed Jesus, for the sake of his death for me, overlooks all my offences against him."

"Is that the way he forgives? Would he treat

a great sinner like me as if I had never offended him?"

"Most certainly. He was crucified for our offences; he bore our sins; he takes them all away, and treats us as if we had always been righteous. This"—the friar spoke very low—"this is what Luther calls justification by faith. Only believe in Jesus, cast yourself upon him, and he will thus forgive and justify you."

"Dare I believe that he will do it? It seems too great a thing for him to do. It is too much for me to expect."

"He died for you, and thus he bought for you a pardon. It is offered to you freely. Believe him, and you shall have it."

"Then I will pray, 'Lord, I believe; help thou my unbelief.'" Again he was lost in his own thoughts, and the friar left him.

In a short time the gospel was to Berthelot "like a loud trumpet sounding the praise of the grace of Christ." He felt that he was "the chief of sinners," redeemed by the only Saviour; a specimen of what the grace of God could do for the guiltiest of men. "Mercy has been shown me," he said, "in order that the love of God, which pardons the greatest of sinners, may be placed before men, as if it were set on a hill to be seen by all the world." He who had once indulged in quarrels now gave himself to prayer and peace. The wolf had become a lamb.

"Father," said he, one day, "I seem to be the happiest man in the city, and yet there are two things which would make me even happier, if I could do them."

"What are they?" asked the older Milon, as he gave one more pull to the waxed threads, and looked up at his son, who had been reading his Testament so quietly that he was supposed to be asleep.

"One is, that I could work again in the shop. It is hard to see you pegging and stitching in order to support me, as well as the rest of the family."

"It is no harder now than it used to be." The old man did not think what an arrow this truth would be to the heart of his son, and he added, "It is not so hard. I'm glad to earn something to make you comfortable."

"Yes, I have always been a burden to you. Forgive me, for I hope God has. And I lie here thinking that I must always be a burden. Then the times grow hard, for if King Francis will have his wars, the poor people must pay the taxes."

"Oh never be troubled about that. I am thankful that we have plenty of custom, even if the students do not come here as they did when you could fit them so nicely that they were proud of themselves. But what is the other thing?"

Berthelot hesitated. He knew his father's prejudices. He knew that the reading of the Testament would have been opposed, if it had not been a comfort to himself. At length he took courage to say, "Friar Bernard says it is right for me to read this little book."

"Friar Bernard is very kind; he likes to indulge you."

"Well, if you would let me read it to you"—The old shoemaker was quite astonished. What need had he of the readings? What would Beda say? The Sorbonne would surely not punish his poor crippled son for making himself happy with the Bible, but if he should listen to it, they might throw him into prison, and then what would his family do?"

"Do let me read the story of Jesus at Jacob's well." He began, and the old man plied his awl and his threads with all his might. After a little he stopped—"What is that? Read it again."

"Jesus answered and said unto her, Whosoever drinketh of this water shall thirst again; but whosoever drinketh of the water that I shall give him, shall never thirst; but the water that I shall give him shall be in him a well of water springing up into everlasting life."

Thus one read the good word, the other listened, and both talked of its beauty and riches. The old man began to be impatient when a customer sat too long, or a lounger hung about the doors. Then he grew bolder, and he would say to those who lingered to tell over the news for the third time, "We have the good news here, and if you want to learn what made the angels sing and sinners shout, just listen to the little book there." The customers began to come almost every day. They formed a sort of Bible-reader's class. In the shoe-shop was taught a sounder theology than in the Sorbonne. Berthelot had his little meetings on a new plan. His musical skill was put to a sacred use. As he played and sang Christian hymns the people, whose numbers and visits increased, were charmed with the praises of God. Not a room in all Paris was so full of interest as the shop of the Milons. The Church of the New Testament was in that house.

Many a day had the little shoes that Berthelot had given the children of the martyred waterman, been worn upon the pavements between the shop and their humble home. They brought flowers to him, and he made them merry with music. They solved certain matters of faith for the older Milon, when they said that they "had a father just as much as ever—only he was up in heaven," and that they knew their "Great Father would give them bread on the morrow, for they would ask him for it the first thing in the morning." They came as little sunbeams, nor did "Grandmother Milon," as they called her, ever let them go away empty.

On one of their visits Berthelot caught a new idea. Why could he not teach the children to write? He had scarcely an equal in this art, and he felt restless to do some good to the poor. Once he had applied his skill to inventing sinful amusements; why not now invent some new mode of charity. He began to teach them to make letters. Other poor children were gathered in, and it was his delight to collect them around his bed, give them verses of Scripture, and show how to write them down. Thus he had his Bible-writing school.

One day Duroc, the sheath-maker, called at the shop. He was the *convener* of the "little meetings," and Berthelot had long known how he went about to whisper here and there and tell people where to assemble. He had a finger tied up, and said that in etching a design upon a sword-hilt, he had burned it with aqua-fortis.

"There is something for me to do," said Berthelot, eager to labour with his own hands, and to earn a little to give to the poor. "Can you get me a job of etching? Now I can turn the flourishes of my pen to some account in inventing designs."

The sheath-maker brought him some work soon after, and Berthelot showed himself skilful in etching, with aqua-fortis on knives, daggers, and swords. The goldsmiths heard of him, employed him, and he executed some unusual things for them. He spent his earnings in helping to support the widows and orphans of martyrs, and others who were poor for the sake of the gospel.

People came from all quarters of Paris to visit him; some to see "the excellent and rare things that he did;" some to hear his singing, and others to learn the way of salvation. Every morning and evening his fine voice was heard singing psalms and spiritual songs, while he played upon some musical instrument. This drew many to the shop, situated in the centre of Paris. Many more came, attracted by the great and sudden change that had taken place in him. "If God has bestowed these gifts upon me," said he, "it is that he might show forth his glory by me." He was the comforter of the poor and the inquiring, but if hypocrites or spies came to him, he drew them near and "launched on them the thunderbolts of God." The chronicler adds, "In short, his room was a true school of piety, day and night, re-echoing with the glory of the Lord." He was regarded as the wonder of Paris.

"Why does not young Calvin come to see us?" said Berthelot one day to his father, when they were talking of having some little sermons at their house.

"Perhaps he does not need any new shoes," was the reply; "and if he does, he knows you could not make them for him." This was not the whole truth in the case. Calvin had been very busy in his studies, in writing a book, and in visiting the houses where he met the friends of the gospel. We shall now see how he came, at length, to preach in the shop of the Milons.

There was in the city a man of "sense and credit," named Nicholas Valeton, who had once been receiver at Nantes. He had met with some good people, who had taught him the truth, and the study of the New Testament had confirmed his

7

faith. If there was a new book in any of the shops he was quite likely to hear of it, or if it was not there, he was the man to give the dealers the title of some new volume that the reformers had just sent forth into a world of book-burners. His taste ran that way, and he had money to indulge it.

In one of the shops he was inquiring, on a day in 1532, for a translation of Seneca's *Clemency*, that had just appeared in Paris. The bookseller said he knew nothing about it. Valeton pointed to the back room, as much as to say, "Perhaps you have it in there. I understand how cautious you shop-keepers are. You have a hidden drawer, out of Beda's sight, for the writings of the reformers." The bookseller shook his head. A pale, studious-looking man entered the shop. Valeton thought he had seen him before, as he might have done, had not fear of the people kept the receiver from the little meetings. The stake had a great terror for him.

"Have you any Bibles?" asked the unknown. The shop-keeper shook his head. "I have been going from shop to shop, but the booksellers look at me with suspicion, and declare that they have not a copy." The fact was that the Bible, lately published, had been eagerly bought up, and the doctors of the Sorbonne had tried to prevent the sale. The unknown took his leave.

Valeton followed him, saying, "I can put you on

the track. Be sure always to find the bookseller alone, and point to the back room, and he will understand you. If these fellows possess the truth, fear leads them to lie about it. But you will find some Bibles in the Latin quarter. I am on the search for a new book on *Clemency*, just published by a brilliant young man named Calvin. I will go with you. Do you know Calvin?"

This was a question that put the unknown to the blush. He managed to say, "I can furnish you with a copy of *Clemency*."

"So you have read it. I am told that it lays a good lesson before the king, teaching him to be gentler towards those whom the church calls heretics." The unknown took from his pocket a copy of *Clemency*, and Valeton was obliged to accept it as a present. "From the author, I suspect," thought Valeton, yet he had such respect for the shyness of the young man, that he did not press his inquiries.

"There is a wonderful paralytic, who will take great delight in reading this book," said Valeton. "I will loan it to him. He always has much to say of Calvin, and especially of a sermon that he heard at La Forge's. He is a miracle of grace."

"Present him with this copy," said the unknown, who was now well known, as he himself perceived. "Say to him that he is in danger of Beda's attention, but he must remember the text at La Forge's. May the Lord strengthen him."

"You do not suppose the persecutors will seize him!"

"His influence is too great for them to permit. They will attempt to get rid of that. The spies and eaves-droppers have heard that noble voice singing the praises of his Lord."

"He intends to have preaching in the shop this very week, if any one will dare give the sermon."

"I dare do it. Tell him to send me word." Other arrangements were made for the meeting, as they came near the bookseller's shop. Calvin found the Bibles which he was seeking for his friend Francis Daniel of Orleans. The advocate wished to distribute them, although he strongly adhered to the Romish church. He had lately offered to secure for Calvin an office in the church quite equal to that of bishop. It was refused.

Valeton parted with his new friend, and on his way home entered another book stall, where he found a fresh volume from Margaret, Queen of Navarre. He caught it up, paid for it silently, hid it under his coat, and hurried home. On reaching his room, he opened a large chest, placed this volume along with many others which were kept secret, and then, bolting his door, he opened "Clemency," and read thus—

"Clemency becomes no one so much as it does a king. * * * You spare yourself when you seem to be sparing another. You establish your greatness when you make the public good your chief care, and employ your power for the safety of the people." "Good!" said Valeton to himself; "what Seneca meant for the tyrant Nero, is excellent for our King Francis. I wish his Majesty might read this sentence: 'Let the king so deal with his own subjects as he desires God to deal with him.'"

It seems that Calvin had hoped that the king would read this treatise. He certainly needed it. He claimed to be the "father of letters," and made some noble efforts to draw learned men into the kingdom. But he was too much under the pope and the Sorbonne. He allowed them to persecute those who sought and found the truth of God. He probably never read Calvin's little translation. If he did, he did not profit by it, and he went on imitating Nero, rather than following the advice of Seneca and his young commentator Calvin.

CHAPTER VI.

SONGS AND SERMONS.

Two young men left the Latin quarter one evening, in 1533, and cautiously took the Rue de St. Martin for the shop of the Milons. One of them was Calvin, and the other was Louis Du Tillet, whose gifts and graces made him a most attractive friend. He was of a noble family in Angoulême; his father and two brothers held high offices under the king. He loved the Bible, but feared to follow it, lest it should lead him from the traditions and worship of the Romish church. He loved the church, and expected soon to be a canon of the old cathedral in his native town, yet he knew that the church was wrong in forbidding Christians to read that holy word of which the Lord said, "Search the Scriptures."

As they walked on, arm in arm, Calvin said, "We ought to bless God for the Queen of Navarre. That preaching at the Louvre is a grand stroke of gospel policy." He saw that his friend was not informed of an event which was creating a stir in all Paris, and he explained. "The king was absent in Picardy, and his sister Margaret resolved to give the gospel a throne during the Lent days. She proposed to have Gerard Roussel, her eloquent chaplain, preach in the churches. But the Sorbonne would not allow that, for he is too good a Christian to suit them. He would preach down the Roman follies and hold forth Christ. It was the custom for them to appoint the Lent preachers, and I supposed they would select some furious and insolent monks, who would make the churches ring with their insults against the truth. At any rate, they would not nominate Roussel. Queen Margaret began the contest with them, but they overcame. They had their small revenge in shutting the churches against her chaplain. She was not to be outwitted in this way. The gospel must be preached, now or never, in some public manner."

"It would have been better," said Du Tillet, "to have thrown a shield over your little meetings, and increased them."

"Ah! this is only taking care of a few house-plants; it is not sowing in the broad field of the world, where the Lord ought to have a great harvest. And yet she adopted our plan, on a larger scale. She opened the doors of the palace, fitted up a saloon and gave orders to admit all who came. I wonder that you did not hear of it, deep as you were in your books. The grand movement astonished the people. The crowd that rushed to hear the first sermon, the other day, was so great that there was not room for them. The queen sent me a special card or I would not have got in. The next day she threw open a larger hall, and the people filled it and the stairway and the next rooms. The third day a still larger place was chosen, and room was yet wanting. The people are hungry for the gospel, and yet we must hold our meetings in private houses."

"St. Paul did the same."

"True, he did when shut out of the Synagogue. But the gospel ought to be preached in every Church, from the meanest chapel up to the Notre Dame. Yet the preaching at the Louvre must do some good. The crowds increase. At the hour, as you will see to-morrow, the bridges and boats will be thronged; the students are beginning to go, and you will see nobles, lawyers, professors, and literary men hurrying to the spot. Yet you will refuse to go, I dare say, for you think the mass is worth more than the gospel. I only wish Roussel would preach more like Paul, and then I would force you to attend."

"I confess that I cannot give up the mass," replied Du Tillet sadly. "I wish I could see as you do. I feel that there is nothing but ignorance and darkness within me. But I cannot leave the Church as you have done. And I am astonished at you, when I think of what a sacrifice you make. You might be promoted and made a bishop. The queen would give you a diocese."

"Folly! Did not Paul count all things but loss, for Christ? Yes, she would never buy me off with a promotion. She told me, one day, that she would like to have me in her service. My reply was, that it is well known how little I frequent the courts of princes, and I thank the Lord that I have never been tempted to seek the smiles of royalty, for I am satisfied with my good Master, who retains me in his household. My dear Louis, you must think less of the Church and more of Christ."

They reached Milon's house. Many persons passing, during the day, had seen a nail driven in the pavement as the signal, and others had been summoned by Duroc, the sheath-maker, so that the rooms were already full. "You cannot get in," said the convener to many of the comers. "Go to La Forge's; he will have a meeting for those who are not able to find room here." When he saw Calvin and his friend at the door, he found a way for them to enter.

In the fervent prayers that evening, there were hearty thanks to God because "Salvation had come to the house." Poor mothers were silently blessing the Lord for what Berthelot had done for their children. Calvin preached on the Conversion of Paul, closing in his usual words, "If God be for us, who can be against us."

There was a deep silence. All eyes were turned to the paralytic on his couch. All wished to hear from him, for they knew his full heart might pour its consolations into their own. He begged to be raised up a little, although the position gave him extreme pain. He began:

"How wonderful is the mercy of Jesus! It has made me a poor cripple. It has brought me to great suffering of body, but what joy of mind! It has made me helpless, and yet I never was so strong. I shall never rise and walk as the man sick with the palsy did, but I do trust that Jesus says, 'Son, thy sins be forgiven thee.' I thank the good Lord for these pains; they are some of my richest mercies. What was I doing before they were sent? Hating you, ridiculing you, despising the Holy Bible, and blaspheming my God. Oh, if I could only pray more, read the good word more, and love you all more! How strange that I—I, who ran after the worst companions—I, who grieved my dear parents—I, who scoffed at your religion—I, who loved dances and revels—should see this house so full of praying Christians. Help me to bless God for this. See what he has done. He wanted to show how great was his love to sinners. So he took the worst of them all, the very chief of sinners, and crippled him so that he could not fight so stoutly against God. And if he has chosen me to be one of his little flock, do you not see how ready he is to save you? I ought to love him, because he first loved me, and does he not love you all? But why do I speak? I fear my words will only do harm to the blessed gospel"—

"Go on," said Calvin and others. He declined. "Sing, sing then for us," whispered his friends, who knew the charms of his voice. "Sing the Queen's

Hymn," said several persons who had lately heard him singing one of Margaret's Martyr Hymns that became very popular afterwards. He began:

O Lord, our God arise,
Scatter thine enemies
    Who thirst for blood;
Death, which on earth doth reign
With sin and mortal pain,
Is everlasting gain
    To men of God.

They, through the shaded vale
Walk firm and do not quail,
    With thee to rest;
The fiery death they face,
And march to that glad place
Where, with the crown of grace
    Thy sons are blest.

Help those who trust thee, Lord,
And give them for reward
    This death of joy;
O Lord our God, arise,
Stand forth beneath the skies,
Subdue thine enemies,
    Who us destroy.

The people had heard of justification by faith, and had seen an evidence of the power of God's saving grace. They were hopeful of great results.

"Paris will be full of our little meetings, perhaps, after a while," said some as they spoke softly on their homeward way.

"And think of the great meetings at the Louvre," was the reply.

"They are not for us," said some. "But we

common people may go to hear the good Courault, as he preaches to immense crowds at St. Saviour's. He can scarcely see to read the Bible, but he causes his hearers to see the truth."

"And Friar Bernard," said others, "tells those who come to his box, to confess their faith there, and confess their sins to God."

A day or two after this, Berthelot's friend, the Sculptor, went to St. Saviour's. His beautiful statue had been admired by lovers of art, and adored by superstitious worshippers of Mary, for many months. Among the crowds that went to hear the great preacher, were numbers who paid it great reverence. Vallette went to see how the people treated it, quite as much as to hear the eloquent Courault. Bashful and shrinking from notice, he stood near Friar Bernard's confession box, watching the people crowding along the aisle by the wall. Many knelt and said their *Ave Maria;* some gazed at the work of art as if it pained them to see a beautiful piece of marble worshipped; and others lent it their scowl. He was surprised to see so many of the two latter classes, until he saw that the people of the little meetings chose this part of the church near Friar Bernard. The heart of the artist was sad, for he thought that to despise the statue was to insult the "Adorable Virgin."

The preacher entered the pulpit; and solemn silence prevailed. His manner was bold, somewhat rough, and intensely earnest. He was alive with the gospel, and did not spare the errors of the Church, nor the vices of its members. "There is one Mediator," said he, "and only one. Is it Mary? Blessed was she in being the Mother of Jesus, but yet she was by nature a sinner. Oh, ye who adore the pure marble that pretends to claim your adoration, know that she was a poor, lost, dying, helpless sinner, like yourselves, until she repented and believed in her crucified Son. I love to think of her, for she would not dare to wear the crown which belongs only to her divine Son and Saviour. The more sinners we see redeemed, the more hope is there for us, if we will believe in Christ. Turn away from that image"—he pointed to the statue—"and look to the true cross of Calvary. There the one Mediator dies for you. Turn away from the saints! They were sinners once, and they went directly to Jesus: Why may not you? Turn away from the mass! Jesus is not in it crucified afresh for you. He need not be. He once offered himself up for you; that was enough. Turn away from all human rites; cease to worship the creature more than the Creator; cease to put the Church before Christ; believe in Jesus, love him, pray to him, serve him, die for him, if need be, and you will be saved. There is no other Saviour. One is enough." And these words seemed to ring among the rafters, "*One is enough.*"

The modest artist was grieved. "So he calls that an *image*," thought he. "Yes, they call it an image. No longer will they call it the Holy Virgin." He felt the eyes of many around him burning upon his face, as if they knew that it was the work of his hands. He wished that his chief work, which was his pride, were back in his shop, where he might hide it from the public view, and that he might creep away from the indignation poured upon it. "These gospellers hate me," said he to himself. He fell back a little, and turned to find some way of escape, or some corner in which to hide. But the aisle was crowded with people. Just behind him were the tall Surgeon Pointet looking over his shoulders, and the short bricklayer looking through him, at the zealous preacher. There too were Calvin and Du Tillet, listening with delight. The words, "One is enough," often repeated, seemed to fill the whole house. The sculptor must breathe that air of life.

"And think who he is;" cried the preacher. "He is the Lord of glory. * * * Think what men did to him. They hated him; they seized, they scourged, they nailed him to a cross. Come up to Cavalry with me. Behold your crucified Lord. He dies once for you all. Then why do you bow to images and little crosses, and thus crucify him afresh? Why do you imagine that every time the priest elevates the host in the Mass, he offers Jesus as a sacrifice again for you? Jesus died once to take away your sins. One sacrifice is enough."

This was good news to many in the Church, and Vallette began to believe that the way of pardon and life was in Jesus alone. He still heard the preacher saying, "Why do you pray to the saints? Why not to Jesus only? He promises to hear you. He will plead with the Father for you. He is the only advocate of sinners. The saints can do nothing for you. You do not need their prayers. One intercessor is enough."

The artist was trembling, weeping, ready to faint and fall. The strong arm of the Surgeon was put forth to hold him up, and his lips whispered, "Believe in the Lord Jesus Christ and thou shalt be saved."

"But I have insulted him. It was my hands that made the image which everybody despises. I have adored Mary and not Christ. I have crucified him afresh. The preacher's eye is fixed on me."

"Listen: hear what the good preacher is saying." Courault, with tender voice, was inviting sinners. "You all may come to Jesus—come now—come all at once. In his hand is the pardon you want. Take it freely. He asks you no price. He paid for it on the cross. At his feet is the true confessional. Bow down there and confess your sins. Go to your homes, and seek some corner where you may kneel and pray for his forgiveness, his love, his power, and his salvation."

The service ended, the preacher disappeared, the people lingered. The sculptor found himself walking with his arm upon that of Surgeon Pointet. "Where is your room?" asked the Surgeon.

"I have none," replied the broken-hearted Sculptor, "except the shop, and I dare not go there. I am too poor to have a home."

The surgeon inquired further into the surprising case, and this was the story of the artist: "I wanted to make some offering to religion. I contributed that statue of Mary. It cost me long days and nights of work. It brought me into debt. Besides that I have been sick for months. My landlord turned me out of his house. I had no bed nor board. The shop became my lodging-place, but no one knew it except my fellow-workmen. They informed my employer. He suspected me of being a heretic, because I said that Tielly, the priest who caused the sad injury to Berthelot, was a bad character. That priest has often come into the shop to accuse me of being a friend to poor young Milon. I could not deny that I was, and that I often visited him. Yesterday they found me reading a book which Berthelot sent me, and they took it from me, saying that I might look for Beda next. No man was ever a blinder devotee to popery than I have been. It seemed cruel to be accused of heresy, when I opposed it with all my heart. I went to-day to St. Saviour's to see my statue once more, and then leave the city, if I could have strength to walk away."

"Come with me," said the Surgeon, whose heart was touched, for he understood that the Sculptor had been almost starving himself, while toiling for a hard master. "My house shall be your home."

"No, sir, thank you; I will first go to see Berthelot. He has suspected that I am in trouble, but I have refused to tell him what it is. He once scoffed at my idolatry; now he wants to tell me of the true worship of Christ."

The Surgeon urged the young artist into an inn, where he ordered a refreshing dinner for themselves, and their talk ran upon the glorious gospel, to whose feast the neediest are freely invited. But who should enter the room with noisy, blustering pomp, but the priest Tielly, calling for the portion of a glutton and a wine-bibber? and who was with him but young Coiffard, whom the priest had cunningly ensnared, that he might have a sumptuous feast at the expense of the wild law-student? On all sides it was a surprise meeting. The timid Sculptor would have been insulted by the rough burly priest, had not the Surgeon's shield been over his head. We shall hear of this scene again, and now we follow Vallette to the house of the Milons, whose door is as widely opened to him as Berthelot's roomy heart.

"That book of yours will condemn me," said the artist, after rehearsing his story. "It will bring the last blow. I will not again venture into the shop. I know one workman who will bring me my few tools and scanty clothing. But where shall I go?"

"Stay here. Of course you will. Protestant art will be needed one of these days. Christians will want fine statues, not for worship, but for their softening influence upon manners. You will come and live here with us. You can invent beautiful designs for the goldsmiths and sword-makers, and I can etch them. We'll set up the business together and defy competition. Cheer up; the Lord will provide. And what talks and readings we will have!"

The Surgeon had not been in the house of the Milons since he had been dismissed at the interference of the crafty confessor. He had to stem the tide of explanations and apologies on the part of the father and mother. His reply was that he was thankful for their conversion to their Lord and Saviour, and they indulged in their joy over the happiness of their poor son who had been such a blessing to their souls.

"It grieves me to have let your book get into the hands of your enemies," said the Sculptor. "I was off my guard when it was found before me on my block. I wish I could read the passages which you had marked."

"Do not grieve. Here is another copy. Friar Bernard leaves me some to distribute." Berthelot took down from a box, which was fixed within his reach, a copy of a book which was exciting no little commotion among the Sorbonnists. It was a poem, published by Queen Margaret a year or two before, entitled, "*The Mirror of the Sinful Soul, in which she discovers her Faults and Sins, as also the Grace and Blessings bestowed on her by Jesus Christ, her*

Spouse." Berthelot opened the volume, and repeated such lines as these, for he had committed them to memory:

Jesus, true fisher thou of souls!
  My only Saviour, only advocate!
Since thou God's righteousness hast satisfied,
  I fear no more to fail at heaven's gate.

My Spouse bears all my sins, though great they be,
And all his merits places upon me. * * * * *
Come, Saviour, make thy mercies known. * * * *
Jesus for me was crucified:
For me the bitter death endured,
For me eternal life procured.

Margaret's poems were not elegant appeals to the imagination, and, in other days, neither Berthelot nor the artist would have considered them worth reading. They were theology in rhyme, but this was just what these two friends needed. Berthelot grew earnest as he recited,

Pain or death no more I fear,
While Jesus Christ is with me here:
Of myself no strength have I,
But God, my shield, is ever nigh.

* * * * * *

How beautiful is death
That brings to weary me the hour of rest!
Oh! hear my cry, and hasten, Lord, to me,
And put an end to all my misery.

"I fear that I am not ready to say so much," added Berthelot. "My miseries are very mercies, and I want to enjoy them until I am more refined in the furnace. They will not be met with in heaven. But do not think they are merits. Do you remember the money I threw down in your shop for the bricklayer to carry to the widow of the waterman?"

"I do," replied Vallette. "I wondered at you."

"I then supposed that such gifts were my merits. I ridiculed your religion as well as that of poor Anthony Poille. I fancied that my charities would save my soul. But now I wish to give charities because Jesus saves me by his life and death. You must now live with me, and help me, and we will both live for Christ." The Sculptor could not resist making his home with the Milons.

CHAPTER VII.

THE FLIGHT OF THE LEADERS.

"PROFESSOR COP will be spoiled," said certain of the Sorbonnists, as they met him, arm in arm, with Calvin, slowly walking through the Latin quarter.

"He might be burned, if his father were not physician to the King," replied others who were angry because Francis would not allow them to drive his sister Margaret from the city to her own little kingdom of Navarre. Her "Mirror" had been declared a forbidden book by the Sorbonne. The king was enraged about it. Cop took the part of Margaret, and strange to everybody, the university elected this young man to be its rector. "Wonderful!" said Calvin and his friends. "The king, his sister, the rector of the University, and even, as some say, the bishop of Paris, all lean to the side of the word of God. How then can France fail to be reformed?"

These were the affairs which the rector was talking over with Calvin as they entered a room in one of the colleges. "Your advice was excellent," said the rector. "The four faculties met to-day, and we had a warm time of it. I told them that they had attacked the best woman in the realm, and pronounced her book a heresy. If it be so, then the gospel is heresy. I said, 'You must take back what you have declared against her and her poems. The prior, who said that she ought to be sewed in a sack and thrown into the river, has been punished by the king. His Majesty ordered that he be treated as he had proposed to treat her, and the people were ready to drown him. But the queen interceded for the wretch, and he has been deprived of his offices and sent, for two years, to the galleys. You have encouraged such abuse. If the queen be assaulted, you will be held as the authors of the deed. The students have ridiculed her in a play upon the stage in the college of Navarre; yet they wipe their mouths and say—It was not we who did it. It was the University. Let the faculties retract, or the king will give them trouble.' "

"And what did they do?"

"They remembered that the king had shut up Beda in prison, and afterwards banished him and his chief agents. They disavowed their former rashness. They laid the blame on Le Clerq, who has searched the bookshops for copies of the poems. He was full of wrath, thus to have their base conduct charged upon him, and to be made the Jonah whom they would force into the sea. The faculties prayed the king to accept their apology."

"Good! Margaret has triumphed over the monks, to the great comfort of all believers. Surely we may hope that a mighty reformation is coming.

The king and the best men about him seem to favour the gospel. Be strong in your high position. Let your voice be heard."

"How can I? I am not a preacher." Cop was educated for a physician.

"Let me tell you. You have an inaugural to deliver on All-Saints' day. Break over the old rule of making a mere formal address in dead Latin. Give the people something in a live language. Proclaim the gospel boldly in the face of all France."

"I am not a divine; I cannot speak like one. But if you will write the address, I will deliver it."

"It shall be done. You know the risk we are running."

"Yes, and I am willing to incur it. What shall be the subject?"

"Let it be the essence of the gospel, under the true title of '*Christian Philosophy.*'" The friends separated.

On All-Saints' day, 1533, a pompous procession moved from the University Colleges, to the Mathurin's Church. The monks took their seats and opened their ears. The students were eager to hear the new rector, who had brought the Sorbonne and other faculties to terms. Here and there through the Church, were scattered many friends of the truth, waiting to see the battle, and very hopeful of victory. At the hour Rector Cop began, as Beza says, "in a very different fashion from what was usual." There was nothing dry and dead in his definition of Christian Philosophy. "It is this," said he, "The revealed will of God; the plan of salvation by Jesus Christ. *The grace of God alone remits sins.* * * * *The Holy Ghost is promised to all Christians.* Sirs, since the dignity and glory of this gospel are so just, how I rejoice to lay it before you to-day."

What! not a word about the Saints, whom the day brought to mind! only one intercessor proclaimed on the festival of *All-Saints!* Jesus the only Saviour, and Mary nothing but his mother! It is no wonder that many of the hearers became uneasy. On a bench apart from the rest sat a young man of humble appearance, calm, modest and attentive to all that was said. He was about the only one who was not surprised, for he had written it all. None suspected that it was he who was to set the whole University, and indeed all France, in commotion. He must have noticed the signs of anger upon most faces, as well as the joy upon his few friends present.

Two Franciscan Monks could scarcely keep their seats, and when the assembly was breaking up they were heard expressing their indignation. "Grace * * * God's pardon * * * Christ the one mediator * * * * the Holy Ghost—there is enough of all that in the address, but of penance, indulgences, and of meritorious works, not a word." The monks consulted together. It was agreed that the University would not give Cop his due punishment; so they hastened to lay the rector's heresies before Parliament. This high court soon condemned the doctrines of the rector's inaugural.

Calvin went home one way, and Cop another, where each was soon visited by friends of the truth. Some rejoiced, others said, "It was a sad mistake. We ought to be contented with our little meetings in retired places."

"No," said Calvin. "Our Lord went into the very temple and proclaimed these same great doctrines, and so did Peter and John."

"True, but Jesus died for it, and his apostles were thrust into prison."

"Is fear to prevail over us?" asked Calvin in his greatest earnestness? "Are our friends going to quail and flee? When the standard-bearer mounts the wall will his soldiers refuse to take the fortress? Then if our enemies seize us and remove us from you, you will deserve to be left to yourselves."

In a day or two Calvin and the rector were together, talking over the action of parliament in condemning the address. "What will you do?" asked its author.

"I will meet the monks on my own field. It is a maxim that all members of the University shall first be tried by the four faculties. How much more is this the right of the head of them all? I will defend the address before them." They formed their plan.

The faculties were convened. "The privileges of the University have been attacked," said the fearless rector. "It has been insulted by allowing its chief to be denounced in parliament. Bring those impudent informers to trial, and make them give satisfaction for the insult."

The theologians, who had hung down their heads when Cop defended the Queen of Navarre, were again in confusion. They could find no scape-goat, and resolved to fall on the rector with all their forces. They raised a loud cry against him. But they made matters worse and worse. They became divided into two parties. One of them shouted, "We must not retreat. We must crush out the heresy that threatens us, or the Romish doctrines will be expelled from among us."

"The gospel, philosophy, and liberty," shouted the other party. "We must rise up and defend the truth." The noise and disturbance became so great that nothing could be heard. At last a vote was taken. The two faculties of law and divinity voted against the rector; the two faculties of law and medicine sustained him. He refused to vote, although it would have given him the victory. Cop must appear before parliament.

Calvin received an invitation to visit the Queen of Navarre. His friends were delighted, hoping that it would result in great good to the Christian cause. "Perhaps," they said, "she will stay the coming storm." He went to the court. She rose to meet him, when he was ushered in, made him sit down by her side, and they exchanged their views.

She looked upon him as the rising leader of the party which would altogether renounce the old Church, and go back to that true Church which was oldest of all. He did not expect her sympathies, for she clung to the Roman Church, while trying to reform its errors. What he gained by the interview we know not. Perhaps he left with a strengthened hope that the rector would win the day.

"Shall I go before parliament?" asked Cop, after they had conferred together. "If I do, then you may be exposed to danger, although I will never reveal our secret, even if they torture me."

"Yes, go; and I shall expect to follow. Our Lord maintained his doctrines before Pilate, and let us not forsake him."

The rector got himself ready to appear, as became the chief of the first university in Christendom. He put on his official robes, and, with a troupe of beadles going in advance, he set out for the Palace of Justice. A large procession followed. When passing through a narrow street, where there was much confusion, a man hurried up and whispered in Cop's ear, "Beware of the enemy: they intend to shut you up in prison. Berquin's fate awaits you. A member of the court—your friend—has sent me to warn you. I have just seen the officers, on another street, who are waylaying you: if you go farther, you are a dead man."

What was to be done? No Calvin was at his side to give him advice. He lost his presence of mind.

The procession was stopped by the confusion. His friends came to him, and amid the disorder, hastily escaped with him. He entered his room, flung off his cap and gown, caught up a few needed articles, and put in his pocket the seal of the University. Some think that he did this by mistake, but, more likely, he took the seal so that it might still be understood that he was the proper rector of the faculties. His friends hurried him out of Paris, and put him on the road to Basle, his native city. The archers came, but the rector was beyond their grasp. The angry parliament offered a reward of three hundred crowns to any one who would bring him back dead or alive. Cop was soon safe beyond the Rhine.

"After all Cop was only the shadow," said his enemies, "we must strike the substance. Calvin is the man whom we must seize."

"Yes," cried certain men like the priest Tielly, "he is filling the heart of the city with his doctrines. We have followed his track as he has gone by night to teach in the houses of the people. Shall we arrest him?"

"Let the Lieutenant-criminal, Jean Morin, seize him," said the parliament.

Calvin was sitting quietly in his room in the college of Fortret, trusting to his obscurity, to the protection of Margaret, and to God for safety. He was in no little excitement about the dangers that his friend had just escaped, but he did not believe that he was worth the notice of the persecutors. His friends were alarmed. Those, who had helped Cop to flee, came in haste, saying, "Fly, fly, or you are lost."

"They surely will not seek for me," replied Calvin.

"They are coming now. There they are now in the street. We will go down and parley with them, while you escape." They went to the gates, but the officers moved on towards Calvin's door. The students had their wits at work; some of them managed to puzzle the searchers; others twisted the bed-clothes into a rope, and let Calvin down into the street of the Bernardins, quite as Paul was let down by the wall of Damascus in a basket.

Morin entered the room just one moment too late. He was always cruel, but perhaps was now too enraged to take revenge on the students. "Chase him," he cried to some of his pack, but they were so bewildered that they ran the wrong way. "Ha! I'll get at the secret of this whole business," said he, as he saw certain papers in the room. He laid hands on them. We shall hear of these papers again, for they exposed certain friends of Calvin to great danger, and even to death.

It appears from the account given by a Canon of the church, that Calvin hastened along the street of St. Victor, to the suburbs of that name. Just where the gardens began to expand into fields, dwelt a vine-dresser, who probably belonged to the band which kept up the little meetings. Calvin went to this honest protestant and told him what had occurred. Having, no doubt, heard Calvin expound the Scriptures, the vine-dresser felt for him the tender affection of a father, and said to him, "If you must flee, change clothes with me." Forthwith it was done, and the young evangelist was soon under a peasant's coat. With a hoe on one shoulder and a wallet slung over the other, and some provisions for the journey, he set out on his way. If Morin and his officers had overtaken him, they would hardly have detected the future reformer in this rustic garb.

Soon a Canon met him; they had known each other. Calvin could not avoid him. The Romanist fixed his eye upon the fugitive and recognized him. He knew what was the matter, for all Paris was full of it. "Change your manner of life," said the Canon. "Look to your safety, and I will promise you a good appointment." The man told this of himself, and then confessed that he regarded bribery or Simony a very innocent offence.

"I cannot be bought," replied Calvin. "I shall go through with it to the last." He passed on, avoiding places where he would be known. Beyond Versailles he came to the mansion of de Hasseville, where he was sheltered for three days, and then passed southward for the lands of Margaret of Navarre, often saying to his weary self, "Never tire in the middle of your journey."

Louis Du Tillet was now a Canon in the old town

of Angoulême, his native place. He also had the parish of Claix under his charge, and when not in it, he was alone in the large house of his father. One day a stranger called at the door and inquired for him. To his astonishment, he found his friend Calvin seeking a refuge from his pursuers. Both were delighted as they warmly greeted each other. Calvin told the whole story of his flight, saying, "And now I come to impose myself upon one whom I can trust."

"I shall count myself the happiest of men," replied Du Tillet, "if I can protect my dear friend from his foes. What pleasant conversations we shall have! I need you for my teacher."

"I need rather to be taught. My chief trouble will be that I shall be away from books and professors."

"Books! You can have plenty of them. Come this way and see." They entered a long hall, where was one of the best libraries in France. "All at your service," said Louis.

Calvin made himself at home. This learned retreat was the dream of his life. He named the town *Doxopolis*, the city of glory. It was his *Patmos*. He complained of his "indolence;" he wrote that his protector's kindness was enough to rouse up the laziest of men. He shut himself up in the library. He passed whole days without eating, and nights without sleep. This was his sort of *indolence!*

It was here that he made certain notes and wrote

out certain doctrines, which afterwards entered into his celebrated "Institutes." As an enemy of the Reform said, "This is the forge, where the new Vulcan prepared the bolts that he afterwards was to scatter on every side. This is the factory, where he began to make the nets that he afterwards fixed up to catch the simple, and from which a man must be very clever to get out." These were really gospel nets to be used by a true fisher of men.

Even when deep in study, Calvin loved to see the library door open, and have his friend come and sit down for a talk. "You study too closely," said Louis.

"Then I must walk. I have rambled over the hills, and felt that in the presence of God's good works, we are overcome with astonishment, and our tongues fail to express his mercy and wisdom."

"Come with me to a vineyard that I have, not far out of the city." They went. Calvin was so pleased, that it became his frequent resort. He talked with the simple-hearted peasants, and they long remembered his visits. It is still called *La Calvine.*

Louis had a brother John (afterwards bishop of Meaux,) who came to his old home. They began to study Greek with Calvin. They all spent some time at Claix, where the teacher was the wonder of the neighbours, who called him *the Little Greek.* Certain priests of the better class were drawn to Calvin. At Gerac, in the old castle, lived a prior, who invited Calvin to come and give his opinions to himself and the neighbouring clergy. The gospel was thus spread through the district.

The missionary spirit filled Calvin's soul. He proposed to go to Poitiers. Du Tillet felt that he could not be parted from his friend; he joined him. A certain garden, and then a cave, became meeting-places for those who loved the truth. Calvin preached for them. When enemies threatened them, they met in houses, barns, and remote places. Three missionaries were raised up; Babinot, a learned lawyer, went to the region of Garonne, praying and preaching secretly, here and there, in humble conventicles. At Toulouse, he brought many students to the light of the truth. Veron went on foot through Poitou and Saintonge, gathering up "the stray sheep of the Lord." He laboured thus for more than twenty years, and was called the *Gatherer*. Veron led many of the students and citizens of Poitiers to the Saviour. In after years these three zealous missionaries visited Calvin at Geneva.

CHAPTER VIII.

THE GROANING OF THE PRISONERS.

WHO was the man that sent the messenger to warn Rector Cop of his danger? This was the first question among all Romanists from the cronies of priest Tielly up to the king and the Sorbonne. Everybody made a guess, but no one furnished a proof. Francis, enraged at the flight of the rector and Calvin, and breathing out anger and slaughter, ordered every measure to be taken to discover him. The search was made, but the gentleman moved among the high courtiers without suspicion. It remained as dark a mystery as the breaking of the image of "Our Lady."

Who was the messenger that rushed into the narrow street and whispered in Cop's ear? The reader will remember the man who gave Berthelot a Testament in return for certain insults poured forth from the shop-window. He was a young lawyer, named Viermey, who could afford to keep a spirited horse and ride him so elegantly as to attract the attention of almost all Paris. When Calvin came to the city and declined the request of the Coiffards to live with them, this fine horseman called to give the new comer a ride. They had studied together at Orleans, and their friendship grew closer by their frequent excursions on horseback. Had not the rector made his office a frequent resort? Had it not been for some other reason than to consult the rich store of old law books? Had not Viermey been seen running very fast about the hour of Cop's escape? He ran in quite another direction than toward the narrow street, but that made no difference. Perhaps he had a pair of horses, at the city gates, for the rector and himself to mount when the escape was made. He and his noble horse were found at Orleans the next day, but what of that? He was arrested. His name was upon certain little notes among Calvin's papers. One of them read, "No knotted straw at the *Black Horse* to-night. Stay at your room until I come. Invite Cop. Danger at Berthelot's. The Sculptor must not remain there. I secured the sale of fifty copies of your 'Clemency' at Orleans. It is making you a name in literary circles, but the Sorbonne will attack you for giving advice to the king."

A scribbled paper of Calvin's was put into his hands, with the question, "Did you ever have a copy of that sent you?" It read thus: "You have some influence among gentlemen of the king's court. Will you try to bring 'Clemency' to their notice? Say to them that Cop has introduced it in his classes. It is not merely for the sale that I ask this, although the book has cost me all my money. I must tax my wits to get some of it back. I hope it will do some good. If the king could have it put under his eye——." (Here the writer had stopped.)

"I received a note something like that from Calvin," replied Viermey.

"What did he say the king would do if it could be put under his eye?"

"He wrote nothing of that sort to me."

"Young man, remember, we have a way of drawing out truth by torture."

"Apply it then; I am ready," answered the accused, in the first tide of his courage. The eyes of the judges were fixed upon him. The awful thought astonished him, but he had more need of strength to calm his indignation than to control his fear.

"Take him to prison. Seize all the papers in his office. Look for the seal of the University." This last order did not produce the effect upon Viermey which the judges had expected. He was not startled nor confused. The Lieutenant-criminal, Morin, hastened to obey the commands. This sort of work was becoming as common as it was delightful to them.

One morning Surgeon Pointet was going to St. Saviour's to hear his favourite preacher, Courault. Sad thoughts oppressed him, and perhaps a sermon might dispel them. Many of his friends, named in Calvin's papers had fled from Paris. He knew a little of his own danger; had he known more he would have hurried away to some retreat where the spying priest Tielly could not have hung upon his path. He reached the church; the door was shut; the crowd filled the street. Where was Courault? Was he in prison? Had he fled? Was he sick from his great labours in preaching?

The people were greatly excited. Troops of archers came and drove them away. "I'll go to Berthelot's," said the surgeon to himself. "He always has the news sooner than almost any one else." His shop had become a sort of head-quarters for the gospel-army.

"The preachers are safe," said Berthelot. "They are simply forbidden to preach in the churches. Friar Bernard is too good to be wrathy about it, and too wise to let the fact be turned against us. Courault and even Roussel have consented to go to private houses and turn their preaching into quiet lectures. Friar Bernard will have one of them here to-night if he can. But they want only the members of the family present. That must include the family physician, especially as his advice is gratuitous, and Vallette the lodger."

"We ought to be thankful, for when one teacher is taken away, the Lord sends another. But what if no leader be here this evening?"

"There will be a Leader here; trust the Lord for that; he will be present."

The shop and parlour received more attentions that day than ever before, for the great and eloquent Courault was expected. Every last and lap-stone were hidden away; no such clearing out of leather was ever known within the memory of Berthelot, who playfully said to his father, "Now do not try to make them think you are not a shoemaker. The story will be in the very air of the shop."

"An honest story then;" replied the brisk old man, who had always opposed sweeping and putting things in order, because he could "never get things straight again." He was placing the shoes on the shelves, and when he found that the boxes would not hold them all, he thought it a good time to buy some more, "so that nobody would lose the sermon by turning to criticise a poor cobbler's work."

Berthelot's couch was overspread with a quilt that had been handed down from his great-grandmother, and brought out only on special occasions. But the pride of all the arrangements was a large cushioned chair, borrowed from the neighbour La Forge, for the good minister—if he should condescend to come.

He did come—the celebrated Courault—at the evening hour. He so preached that Surgeon Pointet said afterwards, "He is as great and earnest in a shoe-shop as in a cathedral. His speech rings with the music of the promises."

As only a family was allowed to be present at each of these little meetings, their number was increased. One preacher would go to several houses on the same evening. The Lord was present with the "two or three gathered together," and others pressed in. The houses began to be full. A mighty work of conversion was going on.

"These lectures are worse than the sermons in the churches," said the Sorbonnists, on hearing of the quiet conventicles. Drunkards had been reformed; thieves had ceased to steal; idlers had become industrious; the poor had been made happy; the outcasts were restored to good morals, and wolves of the old church had become lambs of Christ; yet all this was bad for the Sorbonne. If the preachers spoke so near to the hearts of the people in the little meetings, Rome would lose ground.

"Send out the hounds; the game is plenty," said these hard-hearted doctors. Jean Morin once more took the field. He posted his agents on the corners of suspected streets, that they might ferret out the Bible-readers and exhorters. These spies reported dozens of houses where meetings were held. The officers came upon them, seized many of the leaders and scattered the flocks. Alarm fell upon the people, who said, "we have no teachers; we are poor sheep without a shepherd. Since our guides are taken away, let us seek them elsewhere."

"Flee for your lives," whispered Friar Bernard, (who was not suspected of being so firm a friend of the true Christians,) and Courault and Roussel, who knew not what was preparing for themselves. Many escaped to foreign countries.

The Sorbonne felt the need of Beda, and at length secured his return along with his chief agents in cruelty. He soon said, "It is not enough to put these evangelists in prison; we must burn them.

The flames are the best argument against heresy. It is sure, for dead men never return."

"Let any one convicted by two witnesses be burnt forthwith," the parliament declared.

"Apply the decree to Courault and Roussel, at once," demanded Beda.

"Not so fast," said the doctors. "The king's consent must be obtained." These good men and other preachers were thrown into prison.

"Make one cast of the net and catch the whole of these gospellers at once," said the doctors. Morin went to work; he urged on his troops of spies and officers; they entered the houses, went down into cellars and up into garrets; here they took a father and there a mother, and sometimes both of them, leaving the children to starve. About three hundred of the most innocent citizens of Paris were thrust into prison. When this news spread, the alarm increased. "Really," said the Surgeon Pointet, "this is not much unlike the Spanish inquisition."

Beda was glorying in his success. He could not burn Roussel and his friends without the king's consent. The appeal was made to his majesty. "Nobody is condemned in France," he replied, "without a trial. Beda wishes to burn Roussel and his brother preachers. Very well! let him first go to the prison and put them to silence by argument." This was not what the persecutor wanted; it was easier to burn the chaplain than to refute him. But the king compelled him to go. The blustering Sorbonnist stood face to face with the meek and learned Roussel. One used tradition and all manner of quibbles and ridiculous trifling; the other stated great truths and proved them by Scripture. Beda failed; his friends were ashamed of his ignorance; he could rave but he could not reason; he left the prison cell like a routed burglar, glad to get away. The chaplain was not burnt.

One day the king saw on the table of his sitting-room a little book elegantly bound. A literary friend of the truth had placed it there. The king took it up heedlessly, and looked at the title. It was a "Remonstrance addressed to the king," by Beda and his chiefs while they were in exile. The author was now back in Paris, and this book was the last thing he wished his majesty to see. It was a whimpering, cowardly petitioning for mercy. "Ho! ho! this book is addressed to me!" exclaimed Francis. He read enough to find himself insulted and slandered. Never did a match more quickly kindle the fuel, than this volume fired his anger. "Send those wretches to prison," was his next order. "They are guilty of high treason." Beda and his two chief co-workers were soon in their cells. Still the cruel work went on.

For days there had been gloom at the house of the Milons. No one could tell them what had become of the Sculptor. Pointet was no longer to be seen. One by one, their best friends had disappeared. On a certain day Morin came with two officers; a rough, purple-faced priest had led them to the door, and said, "Here is your man." Suddenly they strode through the shop into the room where Berthelot was lying. "We have come for you at last," said Morin. "Dress yourself."

"That is something I have not done for years," answered the paralytic. "I wish I could obey you."

"Yet you could lie here and teach more heresy than all the preachers put together. Now you can have a chance to try the punishment which you have brought upon others by deluding them."

"Oh! do spare our poor helpless crippled son!" cried his mother, reeling under the blow that had fallen upon her spirit.

"We've spared him as long as mercy has been to our advantage. He has been a fine decoy-bird for us. All we had to do was to notice who came here secretly by night, to hear a chapter or a song. His fine voice has been very charming to our watchers, standing out in the darkness and the storm. Make the best of it. He must learn another tune now. It is nonsense to parley: Sergeants! help him on his feet."

In the most cruel manner they lifted him, tried to compel him to stand, and threatened to scourge him. He took it patiently, remembering Him who was "led as a lamb to the slaughter." They saw that he was really and utterly unable to use his feet. They took a cover from his bed and prepared to place him upon it. "Take the couch;" urged his mother; "it will be easier for you to carry, and will be more comfortable——"

"More comfortable!" growled Morin. "You imagine that we seek his comfort, do you? The rack is what he needs, and he may get it if he does not confess and recant. Lay him there, and get him ready. * * * * Here, you priest, take one of these corners and help carry him."

Berthelot saw that this priest was Tielly. If his human nature could have had its way, he would have denounced the wretched spy until his guilty soul would have been overwhelmed in shame. No man more richly deserved a prison than this profligate priest, whom many called "father," and some of them for natural reasons. In days of strength, Berthelot's indignation had boiled against him.

This shaven hypocrite had first disgusted young Milon with the religion of the Romish Church. It had made him a scoffer and an infidel. Never had his Christian temper been so tried and tested as now. The old nature rose up strongly, but silent prayer brought him another strength. He was calm, submissive, resigned. He ignored the insults heaped upon him. He did not murmur at the rough shaking given him as he was raised from the floor, although his pains were most keen whenever the tenderest hands lifted him, or moved the light couch which had been made to lessen his sufferings. With gentleness and love he bade farewell to the mother-whose lips pressed his own, and to the father who was unmanned by the awful grief. They saw him borne away; they saw that the priest took delight in walking as roughly as possible; they knew that he had pangs which would cause almost any other courageous man to shriek; they felt a horror of Romanism for the first time in their lives, and, crushed with their burden, they scarcely understood how to cast it on the Lord.

In a dark, damp cell of the prison, was lying a young man, who, for four years, had been wasting away, and now was helpless. A new sufferer had been thrown in with him, because the prison was becoming crowded, but he was suddenly removed to another cell. Berthelot was put in his place. There would be an exquisite cruelty in seeing two utterly helpless Christians shut up together, one on each side of a gloomy dungeon, on a little straw that partly covered the cold stone floor. The bearers laid him down, saying, "This is the best we can do for you; help each other if you can." The hinges grated, the door was closed, the key was turned, and the two sufferers were left together. Berthelot groaned as some relief to his bodily pains; yet these groans took the form of prayer. "O Lord, how long?"

Had they ever met? They wished to know. They were not long in tracing points of contact in their lives. They had once met—the reader will remember it—it was when Berthelot left the waterman, and a student was led down by some officers and put into a boat. "I have been for several days with a dear friend of yours," said the young man whom Berquin had supported at college, and who was dying because he was suspected of knowing more about the mutilated image than he would reveal, even under the most horrible tortures. "He has told me so much about your conversion, your charities, your skill, your singing, and your warm heart, that I wished for a sight of you. I thought I should go soon to heaven and there watch for you."

"Who was that friend of mine?"

"He said that he was a Sculptor once, and a bigoted papist. He was just now removed so that you could be placed here. What kindness these persecutors will sometimes do without meaning it. But I am selfish in my choice of you. Pardon me; you would rather have him with you."

"I could not have him at any rate. God has ordered this kindness for each of us."

"Speak softly, or we may be deprived of it. I want you to comfort me, and by your prayers and counsels give strength to my weak faith. Your friend was like a new soldier flushed with the joy of his first great victory; he could not talk like a wounded veteran who would console a poor volunteer dying in the prison of an enemy. I am such a dying prisoner; I cannot look back upon any triumphs in spiritual battles. You know all about wounds and victories, and you can comfort me."

"My comfort is sometimes that Jesus was 'wounded for my transgressions.' When the 'Captain of Salvation' dies to save his army, surely none of his soldiers will complain if they must suffer from the arrows of the archers. And then remember that Jesus lives again and comes to take up his poor wounded followers and carry them in his arms. My comfort, at other times, is that the Good Shepherd laid down his life for this poor sheep, and rose again to take me in his arms and bear me safe to heaven."

"That is what a kind priest has often said to me. He comes almost every day now, and when I refuse to recant, he says, 'Be firm in your faith. Remember that beneath thee are the everlasting arms.' It is a kindness in our persecutors to send such a confessor to us."

"He must be Friar Bernard." They talked long and softly about him, and took delight in thinking that he would visit them in the morning. Berthelot was suffering from thirst. A cup of water was near his companion, but it was of no avail. Neither of the prisoners could rise or even creep across the floor. The paralytic, lying on the hard floor instead of the soft springy couch at home, and having no mother there to arrange a pillow for the night of pain, sang his usual evening hymns, and some time during the dark hours he fell asleep.

The next morning a priest entered the cell. He was not Friar Bernard, as they had hoped, coming to comfort the invalids; but Tielly rudely stalking in to insult them. He had just been appointed their confessor, as an exquisite mode of adding to the increasing sorrows of Berthelot. He roughly asked, "Are you ready to confess your sins and recant your heresy?"

"We confess our sins to God, and what you call heresy, we hold to be the truth," replied they.

"Then take the consequences. Die like fools, if you choose, or be burned as the accursed of the Church."

"One word, if you please," said Berthelot with a calm and gentle voice that almost caused the priest to feel ashamed of his harshness, "I have a confession to make to you. Come and let me take your hand."

"No one can be more willing than I am to hear your confession," replied Tielly, hoping for some retraction of heresy. He gave his hand to Berthelot, who held it for some time in silence.

"I confess to you that before my conversion to God, I once struck you in a fray at the dancing hall. It was wrong. I have prayed that the Lord would pardon that sin. Will you forgive me?"

"What do you say?" The priest began to be uneasy. He tried to pull away his hand.

"I confess also that I have prayed that God would soften our hearts and cause us to forgive each other. I have tried to forgive——you." Berthelot was deeply moved. Tielly was so confused that he could find nothing to say to break the pause. "I confess that I have repented of all my sins, and believed on that blessed Jesus who died for you and for me. Oh, if you would do the same—"

The priest made no definite reply, but soon left the cell in a quite different spirit from that in which he had come. One of the first things that he did was to send some little refreshments to the helpless inmates. Perhaps he had a hand in providing a double amount of fresh straw for them. But he was not seen again for several days. No one entered the dungeon, except the servant who brought them their bread and water. Berthelot told him that his companion would soon die, if he did not receive kind attention, but no one seemed to care.

One night Berthelot was wakened from his sleep by the hard breathing of his friend. He called out to him, but there was no answer. "Oh! if I could only get to you," he exclaimed, but he could not move himself. He called aloud; the halls were silent. What could he do? Nothing—nothing but sing. One struggle of the dying man to speak, assured him that his hymn gave comfort. He sang on through the awful hour; at last not a sigh was heard. The sufferer was dead.

The burial of the corpse brought Tielly again to the cell. After it was over he came to Berthelot saying, "I have tried to get an order for your release, but I cannot without being suspected of having a friendship for you."

"Are we not friends? What can they do? Fear not them that kill the body; fear only Him who can punish the soul for its sins and its refusal to believe in a Saviour." The priest was now willing to hear more of the gospel than he had ever before known. His anguish was that he had been such a great sinner, and especially, such a spy and informer against the Christians. For several days he visited the cell as an inquirer for the way of the new life, until he had the satisfaction of helping bear Berthelot home, with gentler hands than he had borne him to the prison. "This is the work of Friar Bernard," said Tielly to the overjoyed mother. "He has written to Queen Margaret, and she has prevailed on the king to release your son."

The Queen of Navarre had also secured the release of Roussel and Courault, but they could not induce the king to set Pointet at liberty. This good man must die. Tielly fled lest he should be forced to testify against him or be thrust into prison. The Surgeon was condemned to be burnt alive, which was done with all possible cruelty. The decisive charge against him was that he had been seen giving the poor Sculptor Vallette his dinner at an inn, and leading him to the house of the Milons.

CHAPTER IX.

THE PLACARDS.

EIGHT months after Calvin had fled from Paris, he returned and showed himself at the sign of the Pelican, where he was met with a cordial welcome by his surprised friends. He proposed to visit openly many of those who had lately been released from prison, and try to preach publicly.

"No, we beg of you to be cautious," said La Forge, "and not expose your life. The persecution is over for a little; the king has put a check on the Bedists; but do not trust too much to the royal tenderness. Beware of teaching in public; let us have the little meetings again." Calvin yielded to these entreaties, and became the guest of La Forge. The hospitality was bountiful, but Calvin's chief delight was in seeing the constant proofs of piety, charity, and zeal in the household. His name was soon whispered among the faithful, and the conventicles were resumed. On many a happy evening he explained the Scriptures to the people who filled the rooms of private houses. He missed the decided Christian Pointet and the Rector Cop; in their place he saw, at the meetings, some certain other prominent citizens, who in later years were eminent in the Protestant Church of France as labourers and martyrs.

Calvin said that some greater attempts must be made for the spread of the gospel. He must visit the Rhine countries and gain wisdom from the reformers. He prepared to leave Paris to the great grief of his many friends. Du Tillet, unwilling to be separated from him, resolved to go wherever he went. They set out for Strasburg, each having a horse and a foot servant. On the way they halted at the little town of Delme, and leaving the horses with the servants, took a ramble through the streets. When they came back, they found that one of the servants had taken the valise which contained their money, mounted the better horse, and rode away as fast as he could. The thief was not caught. The travellers were in trouble. The honest servant offered them the ten crowns that he had with him, and they managed to reach Strasburg. Calvin afterwards went to Geneva, where he spent a most useful and laborious life, and ended his days as a great reformer, honoured of God, and ever since by the Christian world.

The people, who met together frequently in private houses, talked much of what they might do. They became impatient to see some great victory for the gospel. They said, "We must stoutly resist the attempt to bring back the idols of popery into the Church. We *Scripturists* must not yield to the *temporizers*." The first class were those who followed

Calvin; the second were those who looked to the Queen Margaret, and hoped that her plan of a half-reform would succeed.

"Let us send a man to Switzerland to consult William Farel and other Frenchmen who have fled from the kingdom, and are carrying forward a wonderful reformation."

"Agreed," said they all. "Who will go?"

There was a man named Feret, who was one of the most artless, pious, intelligent Christians among them. He was connected with one of the royal offices. They chose him; he departed for the land of the Swiss, many of whose towns had been won from popery. He bore letters to Farel and his co-labourers, who received him with joy, but heard his story with sadness.

"You have victories here in Switzerland," said he, "because you have brave and bold leaders. You march and take places by storm; but in Paris we have no heroic leaders. We do not see great triumphs. The altars and images are not broken down. The temporizers are afraid to attack popery. The Scripturists are not allowed to hold public assemblies. The king does not protect us. What shall we do?"

"A subject ought not to rise in rebellion against his king," said Farel, "but yet he must obey God rather than men. If the king orders you to support popery you are not bound to do it."

"The gospel and popery cannot exist together

any more than fire and water," said Le Comte, who had been one of Calvin's hearers in Paris, and was now preaching among the Swiss.

"Popery is the fire," said Robert Olivetan, Calvin's cousin; "but how will you apply the water?"

"The mass is the abominable thing," said Farel, in his warm style. "It must be destroyed. You have broken down a few images in Paris, but you have not boldly struck at the mass."

"How can we do it?" asked Feret.

"Circulate the New Testament," said the gentle Olivetan, who was becoming one of its translators.

"Yes, that is the great thing," admitted Farel; "but you must amuse those who will not read it. Some are talking of placards. I approve of the plan. Have a large handbill printed, and let it be posted up throughout all Paris, and all the cities of France."

This plan was finally adopted. There seemed to be no other method of reaching the people. Farel wrote the placard. He could not write without using his trenchant style and thundering eloquence. He made it a bold protest against error. It was printed in two forms; one in placards for posting upon the walls, and the other in tracts for dropping in the streets. Feret took them and hastened to Paris, bearing "the thunderbolt forged on Farel's anvil."

Near the gate of St. Denis, at the sign of the *Black Horse*, was a large draper's shop belonging to

John Du Bourg. This tradesman had not been educated in the schools, nor had he conversed much with the evangelists, "but for all that he had not been denied the wisdom from heaven." He was independent in character and liked to see, understand, and judge for himself. He was a diligent reader of the Holy Scriptures, and he learned the gospel tidings, which are ever too good to be kept to one's self. Forthwith he began to tell his neighbours of his treasures of wisdom and knowledge. He was earnest and unwearied.

Some of his relatives shook their heads in great doubt of him, saying, "That ardour, which makes a great show at the beginning, will soon end in smoke, like a fire of tow." But they were mistaken. The word had struck root deep into his heart and it could not be pulled up. The priests tried their arts, his kinsfolk made a clamour, his customers deserted him, and persecution threatened him, but none of them could move him from the truth.

Let us meet in his house, said some of the men, who were most interested in the mission of Feret, and were impatient to hear the report of their messenger. He laid the placard before them. It seemed very bold when read so near the gates of the Louvre and the walls of the Sorbonne. The brave and pious Courault came forward, saying, "Let us beware of posting up these papers; we will only inflame the rage of our adversaries thereby, and increase the persecution and dispersion of believers."

"Let us be cautious," replied La Forge, "of so squaring our prudence, that it will make us act like cowards. If we look timidly from one side to another and do nothing, we will forsake the gospel and Christ." They discussed the matter at length, and a large majority was in favour of the placards.

"Where shall we circulate them?" asked one.

"All over Paris," said some.

"All over France," replied others.

"And at the same time," added De Bourg, "Let us fix upon a night, choose the men, map out the city, and send men to other cities to do the same." These steps were taken. Every man returned home with a bundle of placards and a package of tracts.

The night came; it was the 24th of October, 1534. The selected men went cautiously about their work, each in the quarter assigned him. They knew that they were risking their lives: their movements were silent and mysterious. When one of them came to a gate, door, or wall that he had before chosen, he listened to hear if any one was coming, if not, he hastily posted up his bill or dropped a tract, and hurried on noiselessly to another spot. During the shaded hours, the streets, the cross-ways, the market-places, the long blank walls, the old tottering fences, the prison-doors and palace-gates, bore one of the strongest protests against the mass ever written. Most of these daring men returned to their homes before daylight, but some hid themselves to watch what would happen at the morning hour.

One by one the citizens came out of doors. They saw the large handbills, went up to them and began to read them. At many a place a crowd soon gathered; hundreds of every class, with friars not a few. Some one would read aloud the placard beginning:

TRUTHFUL ARTICLES CONCERNING THE HORRIBLE, GREAT, AND UNBEARABLE ABUSES OF THE POPISH MASS, INVENTED DIRECTLY AGAINST THE HOLY SUPPER OF OUR LORD, THE ONLY MEDIATOR AND ONLY SAVIOUR JESUS CHRIST.

Many persons made their remarks; some vented their wrath and their threats; some expressed their approval, and others simply their astonishment. One picked up the tract and read, "Every believing Christian ought to be very certain that our Lord and only Saviour Jesus Christ—has given his body and soul, his life and blood for our sanctification, by a perfect sacrifice. * * * * Yet there are wretched priests, who set themselves in Christ's place, as if they were our redeemers, and pretend to offer [in the mass] an acceptable sacrifice to God for the salvation both of the living and the dead."

Another read on the church wall: "By the mass the preaching of the gospel is prevented. The time is occupied with bell-ringing, howling, chanting, empty ceremonies, candles, incense, disguises and all manner of conjuration."

There were other sentences more severe than these—too severe indeed to gain the end desired.

Yet there were paragraphs in which the truth was set forth in tenderness. It must have comforted many secret disciples to read this—"The Holy Supper of Jesus Christ reminds us of the great love with which he loved us, so that he washed us with his blood." Many were ready to say, " et the mass be expelled from the churches, and the Lord's Supper restored."

The morning had not passed before the placards produced an immense sensation. The whole people were excited. Priests and friars went about among the citizens telling the most absurd and false stories; one was that the "heretics" had a plot to fire the churches and palaces. The Sorbonne doctors were most furious of all. They wanted only permission of the king to let Beda and Morin loose again upon the believers in Christ. And what of the king?

Francis was at Blois. The gospel had secretly gained over some of the choristers of the royal chapel. One of them was selected to post up the placards in that city. He was daring and imprudent enough to go to the king's room and put one on his majesty's door. The king found it in the morning and he was enraged. He declared, "Let all the gospellers be seized without distinction: I will exterminate them all." The chorister was arrested, put in chains, and sent to Paris. Parliament was ordered to inflict punishment upon all the "heretics." He offered Morin an increase of salary for life, in order to stimulate his zeal. Parliament met, and declared, "Whosoever shall give information concerning the person or persons who posted up the placards shall receive a reward of one hundred crowns; and all who conceal them shall be burnt."

The evangelical Christians remained silent and hidden in their houses. They knew Morin's detective skill. "What shall we do?" they asked.

"Take flight—escape for your lives," said some. Fathers must part from their families and young men must leave the aged to suffer. Many hastened from Paris.

Jean Morin wanted to find a Christian who would betray his brethren. A bright idea struck him: he would seize one man and then hope to take all the rest in his net. "You know Duroc, the sheath-maker. Go and seize him." It was done.

"Sheath-maker, you are one of the heretics, and what is worse, you are their convener. You know where their secret meetings are to be held. I wish to assemble them: you will lead me to their houses."

"I cannot do it. You order me to prove a traitor to innocent men who have trusted me." Poor Duroc trembled, for he knew that Morin was base and cruel.

"Sergeants! get a scaffold ready. This fellow prefers to be set up for public exhibition." The officers left the room. Morin turned again to the sheath-maker, saying, "You have been the guide of the people to the meetings; it is quite fair that you begin the dance. It shall be made as lively for you as fire can make it. But, perhaps, you will now come to terms and tell me who are the guilty wretches that have made all this disturbance."

The affrighted man dare not say that the excitement would have died away if the monks and persecutors had not made such a noise and stirred up such malice against a few men, who had committed an act of imprudence. He was in perplexity. Would he inform against those with whom he had worshipped God? Would he be the agent in leading them to the flames? If not, he must perish. He saw that he was on the point of being burnt. To save himself he yielded and agreed to betray his brethren. "I will tell you," was his reply, "if you will spare me."

Morin called his officials, and they started upon their rounds. The streets were in commotion, because the *Corpus Domini* (body of the Lord, a mere wafer,) was carried solemnly through every parish in order to wipe out the insult lately offered to the mass. The passion had been turned from the worship of Mary to that of the wafer. The houses were hung with drapery, processions were moving about, each carrying the *Corpus Domini*, as if these were so many bodies of the Lord. Morin thought that these proceedings would help conceal his own designs. The betrayer went before him, pale and ashamed. He stopped, he could not speak, he pointed to a door. The Lieutenant-criminal entered. The startled family protested their innocence. They were manacled and sent to prison. Morin was led by the traitor to another house. Thus he went on in his pitiless course, sparing none, great or small, not even the rooms of the colleges.

By degrees the report of this horrible visitation spread through the capital. It went on in advance of the lieutenant. Many, who were merely friends of learning or pleasure were in alarm, lest they should be seized. Like hundreds of others, Nicholas Valeton kept his watch near the window of his house, to notice when the terrible troops were coming. He saw Morin and his company in the street. He turned to his wife saying, "Here he is; take the chest of books out of my room. I will run and meet him. I will detain him, so as to give you time."

The young wife opened the chest, took out the books and thrust them into a secret place. Morin saw her husband approaching and cried out, "Arrest this man, put him in close confinement." He then went up the stairs, searched every corner, saw the empty chest, but found nothing. He was impatient to try this new prisoner with questions, and hastened to the cell where he had just been thrown. He plied all his arts, but could not entrap the clever Valeton. He grew nervous; he knew that his victim was a man of influence; he feared that if he proved nothing against him, Valeton would bear him a grudge that might bring him into trouble with the king, and he resolved to destroy him in a more crafty manner. He thought of the empty chest, and returned to the house.

"Madame," said he to the young wife in a tone that won credence, "Your husband has confessed that he kept all his books and secret papers in this trunk. Besides, we are agreed; I wish to treat him with great mercy; I see that you are almost broken with griet, but do not fear. If you give a certain sum of money and tell where the books are, I swear to you before God, that your husband shall suffer no prejudice."

This lying trick was the unseen net, in which the young and thoughtless wife was caught. She answered his crafty questions; she told everything, gave up the books, and Morin went away saying to himself, "Good! he hid his papers because he felt guilty of heresy. When I can show that a man suspects and condemns himself, his death is sure." He put his spoils in a safe place and sought other victims. "To the *Black Horse*," said he to his sergeants.

"They are coming," said one of the clerks in the draper's shop. "What will you do?" asked another, looking wildly at Du Bourg, who stood more courageous than amazed. He was seized; the clerks and tailors in the shop loved their master, but no one stirred to defend him.

"Oh! do not put chains on my dear husband," shrieked the wife, who was the daughter of another rich tradesman. She poured forth entreaties that were enough to melt the heart of a Spanish tormentor.

"Nonsense!" he exclaimed. "None of your cries of injured innocence here! Manacles are quite too good for the hands that posted up the placards. Sergeants! take this fellow away, and this disagreeable scene will be ended." He took out a list of names, read off those that came next, among whom was that of the poor bricklayer, Poille.

If there was one man in Paris, who could not be suspected of having gone through the streets on the night of the placards, he was the paralytic. When Morin ordered his men to the shop of the Milons, one of them dared to say, "Do you mean the old man? Surely Berthelot was not one of them; he could not move off his bed."

"None of your wisdom; do you dictate to me?" answered the lieutenant, shaking his sword. "What do you say, Mr. Sheath-maker?"

Duroc was silent. How he remembered the pleasant hours with Berthelot, the etchings, the school in which his little daughter had learned to write and to draw beautiful designs! How he thought of the consolations, which the poor bed-ridden Christian had given to his friends in the furnace, after he had been in prison.

"Speak! said Morin angrily. "Your silence is stronger testimony against that crippled wretch than your words."

"Come on," said the traitor, who fainted and fell on the way. "Good proof of that shoemaker's guilt," said Morin. "Men, take care of this coward; I know the house, for it has long been in my eye. I have been there before."

He entered the shop, like one out of mind, says the chronicler, and foaming with rage. He went into the room where Berthelot was lying, and said, "Come, get up."

Berthelot saw his fierce countenance, but was not terrified. With a pleasant smile he answered, "Alas, sir, it wants a greater master than you to make me rise."

"Sergeants; off with this fellow. Take that box, for it may contain some secret papers." Berthelot was thrown into a larger but a worse dungeon than that in which he had seen the student die. But he had more companions. They wondered at his calmness. Often at home he had shrieked with pain, even when his parents moved him a little; at such times he said, "Forgive me, mother; I forgot what Jesus suffered while he was dying for us." But now when enemies tossed him about insultingly, he was like a "sheep dumb before her shearers." The roughest handling seemed tender. He thought of suffering with Christ. The Lord strengthened him. His holy patience made his companions braver and more submissive. His songs were like heavenly music in their ears.

Morin went on with his cruel work, robbing innocent homes and filling up cheerless prisons. Courault and Roussel were put under lock and key. Queen Margaret was in deep anguish. She met the king at Paris. But he would not listen to her pleadings for mercy. He grew cold and even harsh toward her. Heart-broken she left Paris in haste. She perhaps had learned of an attempt to charge her with the affair of the placards.

Beda was not satisfied to have this charge fixed upon the queen, but it must be laid to her brother, the king. The Sorbonne must rule France, and Beda felt that he ruled the Sorbonne. He would show Francis that his attempt to keep down the power of that body should be now avenged. He would teach the king how to put him in prison or send him into exile. Going into the pulpit he preached a sermon full of invective against his majesty. "If the king did not have these bills posted up," he said, "he is, at least, responsible for them. The favour which he shows to heretics and his alliance with the king of England, are the cause of all this mischief."

"Ho! I am to know who is my master," exclaimed the king when the sermon was repeated. "We shall see who is monarch here. Arrest that vain, blustering doctor of the Sorbonne." Beda was seized, accused of high-treason, imprisoned, condemned, made to do penance in front of Notre-Dame, and shut up for the rest of his days in the Abbey of St. Michael. Thus died in obscurity the man, in whom, Erasmus said, there were three thousand monks.

CHAPTER X.

FAITH TRIED BY FIRE.

"COME back to Paris," wrote Francis to his injured sister. Margaret came. She did not find him so gentle as she hoped. The placards annoyed him. "You want no church, no mass, no sacraments, no priests; nothing but your gospel and these troublesome preachers."

"You are quite mistaken," she mildly replied. "I want the Church preserved. I want to see all Christians united under the great bishop of Rome."

"Why don't you say the Pope at Rome?"

"That would displease some who would enter into the grand union. Let Christ be the one Divine head of the Church. Let the bishops and priests become what the Apostles and early preachers were."

"What now?" the king asked, as he saw her unfolding a paper that Lefevre had drawn up for her. "Some new scheme?"

"It is the 'Seven points of the mass,' as the mass ought to be. It says—Let the mass become a *public communion* as was the Lord's Supper at the first. Let not the priest uplift the host (wafer;) nor the people adore it. Let the priests and the people take bread and wine together and celebrate the death of the Lord. Let there be no adoration of images, nor of the Virgin, nor of the saints. Let priests have liberty to marry."

"What then will be left of the mass? Your plan is just that of the placards."

"The mass will become the Lord's Supper; the delight of all true Christians. And just think, my dear brother, who so often came down from his powerful throne to listen to his poor unworthy sister —think what glory it will be for you to unite all sects and restore the unity of the Church, broken for so many centuries. You will not only be hailed in coming time as the 'father of letters,' but as the restorer of the Church in France."

Francis was flattered, shaken and softened. He saw great difficulties, however, in the way. He had given his hand to the pope and his heart to the Medici. Margaret begged him to send for Roussel, Courault and Berthaud—the last had been all along one of the three great preachers. The king was curious to hear how they would solve his difficulties, and he sent for them. They were led out of prison, and Margaret presented them to her royal brother. As she left them she was overjoyed. "Those placards which threatened to ruin everything," thought she, "may perhaps save everything." She was to be deceived.

The three eloquent preachers were not so full of flattery. If they knew of Lefevre's "seven points," they had not much confidence in their success. They were zealous for the truth. They pointed out the errors of the mass, as if they meant to defend the placards. The king was displeased. He sent them back hurriedly to prison.

Two weeks had passed since the first morning of all this uproar and persecution. Seven prisoners were brought before their judges; among them was poor, helpless, but happy Berthelot. The placard had been found in his box among other papers. If his hand had posted up none of them, his heart was in the work. All these seven had their property confiscated. They were condemned to do public penance and be burnt alive on different days. By keeping up the fires for a longer time the court hoped to increase the terror of heresy.

Three days after the sentence, one of the turnkeys entered Berthelot's cell, lifted the paralytic in his arms, carried him forth, threw him into a cart, and drove on to the Grève. A procession followed. As he passed in front of his father's house, Berthelot greeted it with a smile. He waved his farewell to his parents and pointed to heaven. He commenced singing one of the hymns that the passers along that street had so often heard. If he could have had his musical instrument he would have played it as he sang.

"Lower the flames," said the officer in command, "the sentence declares that he is to be burnt *at a slow fire.*" This was done, and the fierce men, who took him from the cart were in haste to lay him upon the smoking pile.

"Will not one moment be given for a confession?' asked Friar Bernard.

"That friar ought to be with him," cried certair monks. "He is as bad as any of them."

The friar dared not say what was in his heart, but the pressure of his hand told volumes to Berthelot, who said, "I do confess—."

"Hear! hear!" cried the monks and doctors, "A recantation. Yes, poor man, it is never too late; go on with your confession."

"I confess that when I stood on this spot a few years ago, and sang to a poor waterman, whom you made a martyr, I was not a believer in his Redeemer. I was a very reckless, wicked man, but you found no fault with such a Barabbas as I was. You wanted to burn only good men. I hated the doctrines of the gospel; I did not then think that I should ever be counted worthy of this glorious death. I have suffered with Jesus; now I am going up to reign with him. I confess that I have not been so calm and patient as I ought, in my sufferings; I wish I had done more for the poor and for the name of Christ. May the Lord make this death a blessing to you all."

The spirit of the paralytic was released from its painful prison, and the body was soon in ashes. Enemies were surprised; friends were strengthened in the faith. With deep emotion they said to one another, "Oh! how great was the constancy of this witness to the Son of God, both in his life and in his death."

"How much good he did to the poor! Do you know that he succeeded in his plan for regaining the property of the waterman's widow?'

"We wondered what had become of her. We supposed this last persecution had driven her away or sent her to prison."

"When the young lawyer Viermey, was in prison, he met with a witness against the men who robbed the waterman of his home in Meaux. After their release they came to Berthelot. He urged them to carry the matter before the Queen of Navarre. She laid the case before the king. He said it was Beda's work, and he would undo it all. The widow is at her old pleasant home now, and you may be sure that the aged Milons will never want for any earthly good, if she can aid them."

"And Viermey has taken the widow to wife," added one, "as if he were living in good old Bible times when marriages were mentioned without any thought of romance. If the persecutors threaten him and his family, you may be sure that he will have fine horses enough to carry him across the border to his friend Calvin."

The next day it was for the wealthy and decided Du Bourg to suffer. All the tears of his wife, entreaties of his friends and appeals to the king had failed to save him. He had counted the cost when he had posted up the placards; he was honest with God in paying it. Among various insults, he was made to walk in sight of his own house, with a taper in his hand and a cord around his neck. From his windows, his friends might have seen the cruel foes cut off that hand, which not long before, had fixed the protest against the mass upon many a wall. He was firm to the end, while being burnt alive. Next came the bricklayer Poille, who was taken to a new place, in order to edify the Romanists of that parish by the sight of a burning heretic. When he was speaking boldly in the name of the Lord Jesus, his persecutors said, "Wait a little; we will stop your prating." How they pierced his cheek and tongue, is too horrible for us to relate. He spoke no more, but his face was all written over with expressions of peace and hope.

We shall not fully reproduce the record of these many martyrdoms. There are some persons in our day who will not believe that the Romish Church is the same in her spirit now that she was in those times of blood and fire. They are offended at these testimonies to her ancient cruelty. They will not believe that she has lately been as cruel in Madeira, in Italy and in South America as she dared to be. They want to hear smooth things of Rome, whose efforts are now unsuspected by many and almost incredible to all, to establish popery in our own land. They will not see the papal errors. They tell us that our liberties cannot be injured by her power.

But whence came those liberties? Through the same Bible for which these martyrs died in the sixteenth century; through such men as fled from Paris and took refuge in Geneva and Switzerland; through such reformers as Calvin, his cousin Olivetan, his old teacher Mathurin Cordier, and scores of heroic men who fled for their lives from France. True protestant liberty followed in the footsteps of the bleeding Church of Christ, and if we pause to note a few, out of hundreds, who gained victories for us in the flames, let none suppose that we take pleasure in the sight. It is painful to write of such scenes; it tries the heart to read of them, but it strengthens our faith to behold the triumph of the martyrs. It helps us to appreciate our glorious gospel and our privileges in the Church and in the republic.

Queen Margaret's entreaties secured the release of numerous prisoners. Among them were Roussel, who retired to his abbey at Clairac, and afterward became a bishop; Berthaud, who resumed the dress of a monk and died in a cloister, and Courault, who would not yield, as his brother preachers had done, to Rome. He escaped from Paris, and, though almost blind, took the road to Switzerland, where he laboured with Farel and Calvin.

The months wore away; in mid-winter all Paris was astir. The burnings had become common; they were a matter of course and had not kept up the crowds in the various parishes. Some new pomp and parade were needed. The king wished to have processions and the streets made imposing with drapery. By solemn marches and public masses he might convince his accusers that he was "the eldest son of the Church." The displays began on the 21st of January, 1535. At an early hour the streets were full of people; the roofs of the houses were almost covered with spectators. The like had never been seen before. Processions moved from place to place; on altars in the streets the priests offered "an expiatory sacrifice"—that is, the mass. Tapestry hung over the doors of the houses, and the windows were filled with pictures. Before each Romanist's door was a lighted torch, "to do reverence to the blessed sacraments and the holy relics." Never before had there been such a display of relics of the saints.

Friar Bernard had never felt such disgust of Romanism. He had kept his real faith a secret, in order to prove the comforter of God's hidden ones. He went with some of the processions from six o'clock in the morning until noon; then he slipped away to visit the prisoners, who were quite forgotten by the bigoted priests, so busy in deluding the people.

"Really this is a happy place," said he to Valeton, as he entered the cold gloomy cell. "I have just been where the scenes must make any Christian miserable. The streets seem paved with human heads. There is not a beam or a stone, jutting out from the walls, but has somebody upon it gazing at the fooleries of the Church and the mockeries against God. They have set up an altar in front of the old shop of the Milons. They do not seem to know that those aged parents of the martyr Berthelot have fled to Meaux. Viermey and his wife take care of them."

"Let us bless God that they remain true to their faith in Christ. They will greatly miss you."

"Not very long; I will follow them as soon as you and your friends here are released."

"Released by death, you mean. I will try to bear the trial. But oh! my wife; has she gone back to the priests and to the old popery? They have used every crafty art with her."

"She has conquered at last. She is safe with the firm Madame La Forge. She sends you every assurance of her faith. If her father rejects her, the Lord will provide for her."

These friends talked a long time upon these serious matters. But the passing events were brought up again. Said Friar Bernard, "I saw two different bodies of St. Matthew to-day. Surely the Church is richer than ever was the Saint himself in this respect."

"They might have a dozen if they had only ordered them," replied Valeton. "I have read of one body of St. Matthew at Rome, a second at Padua, a third at Treves. And so of almost every saint; Europe has plenty of each."

"At one corner some canons stood and cried as

they held up a bottle, 'Here is the milk of the Virgin!'"

"A precious relic! Go to almost any petty town or wretched convent, and you will find it. You might collect it by the quart."

"'Here is the crown of thorns! Blessed are they who adore it,' cried certain monks at another corner. The deluded people trod upon each other to see it. This relic has never before been seen in any procession in Paris."

"I have seen two or three of them in other cities, all at the same hour, and no two alike," answered Valeton. "They exist by scores; it would take a whole hedge to make so many."

"Another train came noisily along, shouting, 'Here is the real cross.'"

"Plenty of them also; I have seen several, each of a different sort of wood. There are cart loads of pieces scattered about among small villages and paltry chapels, to say nothing of the great cathedrals. And the nails of the cross would fill barrels, if they were gathered. I am so thankful that the Lord has delivered me from these superstitions, that I am willing to die for the truth."

Friar Bernard turned the conversation to the comforts of that grace which has always been sufficient for the people of God. He was praying with the prisoner when the turnkey rudely opened the door. Morin entered with his sergeants, saying, "You are wanted at the Marksman's Cross."

"Are you not mistaken about the man you want?" asked Friar Bernard. "This is Nicholas Valeton, who has been promised several days to prepare his answer to the charges founded upon his papers."

"What!" roared the lieutenant, "do you assume to direct me? Come, sir, you are not so free from suspicion that you can afford to be impertinent. We are not bound to keep any promises with heretics. The king is at the Marksman's Cross with his train, and he must have a sight worthy of his eyes."

Valeton and two others were hurried out of the prison. The people in the streets were so excited by the displays they had seen and the speeches they had heard as well as by the king's presence, that they could scarcely keep from tearing these Christians in pieces. The guard appeared and drove them back. Valeton was first brought before the pile. There were his books, which the king ordered to be burnt with him. The wood of the pile had been taken from his own house, as a refined cruelty that might affect him. But this sort of insult did not move him. He saw a new machine of torture before him. It was a pole, like a well-sweep, for raising a man up, swinging him over the flames, and letting him slowly down into them as often as the people demanded. Even this *strappado* (a Spanish invention) did not terrify him. The priests knew that he had never been so active a Christian as many others, and they hoped to make him recant. They said, "We have the universal church with us; out of it there is no salvation. Return to it; your heresy is destroying you."

"Nay; my faith will save me. I only believe in what the prophets and the apostles formerly preached, and what all the company of saints believed." The good people, who came to see their excellent friend, admired his firmness. It was a comfort to him to see them. He and they were thinking how great would be this bereavement to his wife, who was but a recent convert to the faith. The strappado was used; again and again was the firm Christian let down into the flames, until at last the fiends had done their hideous work. This was an atrocious sport to him who was called "the most Christian king!" Romanists have praised him for the coldness and heartlessness which he manifested as a spectator. A Jesuit said, "The king wishes to draw down the blessings of Heaven, by giving this signal example of piety and zeal."

A heathen emperor had once said to the officers, who were putting Christians to death, "Make the wretches feel that they are dying." The Catholic king, Francis I., carried out the cruel edict, seeming to enjoy it with his court, very much as savages do when they burn their prisoners. He ordered the two others, who had been brought out with Valeton, to be swung over the fires by the unhuman *strappado*, and then cut down into the flames. But these three martyrs at the Marksman's Cross did not satisfy his majesty and his courtiers. "To the Halles! to the Halles!" was the cry, and a mass of people rushed thither expecting a second entertainment of a similar kind. The king and his train of nobles had scarcely reached the spot, when the frightful strappado was set in motion. A rich fruit-merchant of the Halles, highly esteemed in all that quarter, was made a victim. Two others followed. The king and court witnessed their convulsions without a shudder, nor did they cringe with horror as the burning pile sent forth its awful odours upon the air. There were, doubtless, many Romish spectators, who felt for the intense sufferings of the innocent Christian martyrs, but there was no evident sign of compassion; the best of them suppressed their tenderest emotions.

Francis returned to the Louvre, satisfied for the time. The courtiers around him declared that the triumph of the "Holy Church" was for ever secured in the kingdom of France. But the people were not so calm; they displayed a cruel joy; they felt a thirst for blood which could scarcely be assuaged, and which would appear again in later years, and in other centuries. Passing over the massacres of 1572, we find another *twenty-first of January* in French history. The date is remarkable. We do not assume that there is any judicial connection between them. But on one of them, Francis First was devoting to death a most innocent part of the people; on the other, four hundred and fifty-eight years later, the people were executing Louis Sixteenth, the most innocent and generous of the Bourbons. In the latter case, vengeance against the throne was not designed by the people, for the awful day of 1535 was not in their minds. Nor were they the protestant descendants of the martyrs, acting in the name of Christians, who made the twenty-first of January, 1793, a day of blood. But, perhaps, the Righteous Judge meant to teach, that where rulers destroy the people for their faith in God, the tide may one day turn in retribution upon their successors. France was destroying the very foundations of the throne, which Louis would vainly strive to make secure.

The king and his officers felt some little vexation; certain nobles, professors, priests, and citizens were not to be found. They were condemned, and their goods confiscated. They were called *Lutherans;* they were such men as Cordier, Calvin, and Courault. One of them was the poet, Clement Marot, who wrote from a foreign land to the king, thus:

> They call me Lutheran—a name
> I have no right to wear;
> Luther came not from heaven for me,
> Nor did he die upon the tree,
> My sins to bear.

This poet was to give to the Reformed Church of France, which rose up a few years after in great glory, the versions of the Psalms that were sung everywhere in the land. Calvin was to go to Geneva, and with his pen give to France, and the Christian world a theology. Marot touched the harp of David, and thousands rejoiced with song: Calvin opened the writings of Paul, and the true faith spread through the world.

Among the quiet scholars, who might have felt that they were safe from persecution, was John Sturm, one of the first modern teachers, who adopted the plan of making philosophy clear to his pupils, and had a simple method of instruction. In his earlier years he had worked at the printing-press, and also had become an author. He went to Paris in 1529, to sell his books. He studied law, then medicine, and afterwards devoted himself to classical literature. A doctor of the Sorbonne, one day, asked him to explain something in the Epistle to the Romans. He commented on it as he would on the letters of Cicero, for he knew not the Scriptures. But a Swiss friend paid him a visit and showed him the writings of Bucer. He read them. He was interested in the doctrines of the Reformers. He was one who crowded in among the hundreds that went to hear Gerard Russel, at the Louvre. He found the gospel and believed. The king gave him a professor's chair in the Royal College, where he grew famous for learning and eloquence.

The placards came; he condemned them. Burnings and banishments became the order of the day, and he trembled. Broken-hearted at the sight of such woes, he abandoned his labours. Many of the martyrs were his friends; they had eaten at his table. In his house, equally open to the shelterless, or the social, he had extended a large hospitality to many who had fallen under the ban of the enraged king. Even if he felt no personal fear, he seemed to expect a general breaking up of all literary enterprises. Who would ever come to study in a city where liberty of thought was forbidden, and where Bible-readers were burned? He was cast down when giving his lessons at the College. Before his eyes were the constant glare of the flames that had reduced to ashes those whom he loved. It seemed to him that barbarism was about to extinguish the torch of learning, and once more overturn society.

"Where are the brothers Duval?" he asked, one day; "one of them the keeper of the privy-purse, and the other the keeper of the lodge in the great park where the king drives and hunts?"

"Gone in haste," replied Gaspar Camel, a nephew of William Farel, "and two clerks of the treasury have fled. Some are hiding in the villages, and others have hastened out of the kingdom. The best servants of the king are no longer favourites."

"I shall go to Strasburg at once," said the professor.

"And I to Dauphiny, my romantic home, where I can hide among the mountains. Wherever we go, we will find company enough, for the people are hurrying along every road in France."

"But where shall we go?" asked scores of humbler ones who knew of no friends to give them refuge. Many went out not knowing whither they went. They could carry nothing with them, but the spirit of faith and forgiveness. They were sometimes obliged to hide themselves in barns and woods, disguising themselves in coarse garments, and enduring hunger and thirst, in order to elude their enemies. Among them was the sister of Berthelot Milon, who could not bear to remain in the city where her helpless brother had been burned.

The learned John Sturm went to Strasburg, where he was yet to add to his good fame and influence by giving the best instruction to youth. He at once sat down at his desk and poured forth his sorrows to Melanchthon. "Oh, what uneasiness," he said, "what anxiety, must not your heart feel in this hour of furious tempests and extreme danger! We were in the best, the finest position, thanks to wise men; and now behold us, through the advice of unskilful men, fallen into the greatest calamity and supreme misery. * * * In the midst of these great and numerous evils, there is only one hope left—that the people are beginning to be disgusted with such cruel persecutions, and that the king blushes, at last, at having thirsted for the blood of these unfortunate men. But we do not despair. God reigns. He will show us the port where we can take refuge; he will give good men an asylum *where they will dare speak their thoughts freely.*"

From this time the French king no longer showed the same favour to men of learning, and especially to that learning which embraced the gospel. He hated such doctrines as had been placarded on the door of his palace, and grew suspicious of everything connected with the Reformation. Protestantism must perish, unless God should intervene and restore what man has sought to destroy. "I am determined," wrote the king to the protestant princes of Germany, "to crush these new doctrines, and to check this disease, which leads to frightful revolts, from spreading further. No one has been spared, whatever his country or rank."

Already had he assembled together the nobles and clergy of Paris, and said to them: "I have summoned you to beg of you to put out of your hearts all opinions that may mislead you * * * and if you know any person infected by this perverse sect, be he your parent, brother, cousin, or connection, give information against him * * * If I saw one of my children defiled by it, I would not spare him * * * I would deliver him up myself, and would sacrifice him to God."

The king paused—wept. The hearers burst into tears. With voices, broken by sobbing, they all exclaimed: "We will live and die for the Catholic religion." Better have wept at the Marksman's Cross!

Francis the First, the "father of letters," ordered that no printing should be done in the realm without his license, under pain of the gallows! This savage edict was not carried out, because the Reformation was toc strong for tyranny to prosper. He commanded all the parliaments to root out the "heresies," but this was not done, for God was raising up that glorious church, which was, in another age, to furnish the victims of St. Bartholomew's day.

One day in February, Stephen La Forge, Calvin's friend and host, was dragged in a cart to the scaffold. He was sixty years old, and some pitied him, saying, "He is a rich man, a good man, who has given away much to the poor." It did not matter; he was burnt alive. Three days later a goldsmith, a painter, and a sculptor had a wonderful mercy shown them. The king wished to see the arts flourish; these three men should not be slain. They should only be beaten within an inch of death, deprived of their goods and banished! The sculptor was Vallette.

"How shall I find my way to a refuge?" exclaimed the timid sculptor, who was allowed three days to remain in the city. "I have no goods to sell; my purse is empty. I dare not apply for work in the villages, and I cannot beg." He almost wished, sometimes, that he might have been put to death.

"Recant, burn your heretical books and make a full confession to the priests," said one of his former companions, who had turned back to the old way, and who knew that Vallette was in deep distress. "The king has shown more mercy to you than to others, because he values your talents. He will gladly pardon you, and then you may become a great artist, and gain the height of your ambition."

"Recant! Burn my Testament! Never—not for my life!" answered the sculptor, repelling the insult to his honour, and to the sincerity of his religious faith.

"Be careful; one in your condition must not think aloud on the corner of these streets."

"Yes, I must be on my guard before men; I know not who may betray me. But I do not fear that my words will be offensive in the sight of God, when defending his holy religion. Silence has been enjoined upon me; already I have laid myself liable to a new arrest. But, dare you betray me?"

"No; not for the world. You have been my kindest friend. You got employment for me when I was almost starving. I want to save you from being a wanderer over the earth."

"And that at the expense of my religion—my very soul! It cannot be. I choose rather to suffer affliction with the people of God. I prefer to be among those, who, my Testament says, 'had trial of cruel mockings, and scourgings, yea, moreover, bonds and imprisonments. They were stoned, they were sawn asunder, were tempted, were slain with the sword; they wandered about in sheep-skins and goat-skins, being destitute, afflicted, tormented; of whom the world was not worthy; they wandered in deserts, and in mountains, and in dens and caves of the earth.' I would rather be like my blessed Lord, who had no place where to lay his head, and who was betrayed by a courteous Judas, and put to death for us, than to have the favour of kings and the cruel mercies of a persecuting church."

"Not sc loud, my friend, or you will betray yourself. You do not know but that every other man who passes by is one of Morin's detectives. Let us walk."

"Whither? I was only venturing out a little to see if I could find Friar Bernard."

"Come, then, I will show you where he is. Not ten minutes ago I saw him enter the house of your excellent friends, the La Forge family. They are overwhelmed with grief. Jeanne is scarcely expected to live."

Vallette was agitated. He walked on in silence. He had been in prison, and he only knew that Stephen La Forge had been suddenly executed. His thoughts had turned to that generous family as soon as he was set free. He wished to thank them, and bid them farewell, expecting never to see them again. His feet had led him to the door, not an hour previously; he had lingered, seen the windows darkened, suspected that family had fled, or feared something more dreadful. His diffidence had prevented him from making any inquiry at the door. The two young men now came near the house.

"We are just in time," said Vallette's guiding friend, "for there is Friar Bernard standing in the door. Catch his eye, and I will leave you."

"Is it possible?" said Friar Bernard, stepping upon the pavement and grasping the hand of the sculptor, when his friend went on his way. "Are we to see you once more before you set out as a pilgrim and stranger, seeking a rest—that rest which remains for the people of God?"

"Come in thou blessed of the Lord," said Madame La Forge, using the salutation which was so often on the lips of her martyred husband. "Friar Bernard will come also, and point out to you the words of comfort."

They were soon seated in the room which had often been filled with God's hidden ones, who there had renewed their vows to God, their pledges to one another, and their spiritual strength. In tears they spoke of the past, and in gloom of the future. "Remember," said Friar Bernard, "that our Lord declared, 'Blessed are they which are persecuted for righteousness' sake; for theirs is the kingdom of heaven. Blessed are ye, when men shall revile you, and persecute you, and say all manner of evil against you falsely for my name's sake.'"

"How often," said Madame La Forge, "did our Calvin close his sermons with the words: 'If God be for us, who can be against us?' And my young friend you will be glad to know that we have just heard of the good leader of our little meetings."

"Does Calvin dare to write to any one here?" asked Vallette.

"Not yet; we will have letters, however, if we remain in this city, as soon as there will be less danger of their being found, and thus involving his friends in new troubles. He does not forget us. A courier, who is not suspected, has seen him at Basle, and he brings us his messages of sympathy."

Calvin had heard of the martyrdom of many of his friends. He grieved to think that certain of them had been implicated in "heresy" by the papers left in his room at the college of Fortret. And the remembrance of their hospitality brought him to tears. How often had he sat at Du Bourg's table, shared in the generosity of La Forge, and conversed with the poor cripple! He thought day and night of the cruel work going on in Paris. He resolved to do something to turn away the sword that threatened other lives. "If I do not oppose it righteously, and to the best of my ability, I shall fairly be called a coward, and disloyal to God on account of my silence. I will reply to the wicked tales that are circulated against my brethren; and as similar cruelties may be practised against many other believers, I will endeavour to touch foreign nations with some compassion in their favour." Such were some of the reasons which led him to shut himself up among his books and write the *Institutes of the Christian Religion*—a work for which he had been long preparing. Never did a noble book have a nobler origin. As he wrote the first pages of it, he was thinking of the extreme sufferings of his faithful brethren. In another work, he said: "The memory of the late Stephen de La Forge ought to be blessed among the faithful as that of a holy martyr to Christ."

How much was there to be recalled concerning him by those who still remained in Paris! Nor did they alone remember him. Let us notice the picture drawn of Calvin in Paris, by a Roman Catholic of a later day. Pasquier says of him: "Devoted otherwise to his books and his study, he was unweariedly active in everything that concerned the advancement of his sect. We have seen our prisons gorged with poor, mistaken wretches, whom he exhorted without ceasing, consoled or confirmed by letters; nor were his messengers wanting, to whom the doors were open, notwithstanding all the diligence exercised by the jailors. Such were the proceedings by which he commenced, and by which he gained, step by step, a part of our France." No wonder that he had warm friends in Paris who talked of him with tears.

"I wish I could follow him," said Vallette. "Perhaps Basle could furnish some work for a poor sculptor."

Why can you not go?" inquired Madame La

Forge, "although we should part with you in sorrow."

Vallette did not like to confess his poverty. Friar Bernard understood the meaning of his silence, and said: "You shall have the means. I have something to share with you. I must keep enough to help myself away when I find that I am suspected of heresy, or of aiding those who love their Saviour and his gospel. My time may soon come."

"And I shall be most happy to assist you, for you may do us a favour. We will leave the city as soon as Jeanne is able to go. Viermey, who often is here, will dispose of our property. You can look us out a home in some of the towns along the Rhine, or in some valley of Switzerland, where the Reformation is established, and we will follow you." Vallette took courage, and left Paris the next day. He was cheered by the hope of benefiting his friends.

The next week Friar Bernard visited a young Italian, who was condemned to the flames. He saw the martyr's wife refused a parting word; she went home, and shortly after, "died of grief at such infamy."

About the same time two ribbon weavers came to Paris from Germany, bringing with them a Lutheran book. They stopped at an inn. "Landlord," said one of them imprudently, "take care of this book, while we go into town, and do not show it to anybody."

"It shall be safe," was the reply. The travellers took their round through the streets. The inn-keeper was curious to know what sort of book had been entrusted to his hands. He turned it round and round, tried to read, but it was all German to him. He went out and showed it to a priest.

"It is full of heresy," said the priest, after opening it. "It is a damnable book. You cannot do a better service than to have its owners arrested."

"I'll send word to Morin." In a short time the two innocent travellers were seized, condemned to have their tongues cut out, and burned, "alive and contumacious," says a journalist of that day.

Paris was not the only place in France where such cruelties were visited upon the innocent Christians. A poor girl had been in service at Rochelle, where her master had taught her the good news of salvation. She returned to her native town in Vendée. One day, a gray friar was preaching there, and she went to hear him. After the sermon, when none others were present, she said to him, "Father, you do not preach the truth."

"How do you say?" he replied. "If you are so wise, point out the truth to the preacher."

"Here it is in the word of God." The friar was ashamed, confused and angry. He could not very well bring charges against his instructor, for there were no witnesses present. But he laid his plot. He preached again. He resolved to get himself reprimanded a second time in the presence of other persons. He insulted the doctrines of grace. The poor girl was so indignant that she said: "If you insult the gospel, the wrath of God will be against you."

"There is another wrath now due to you for insulting a priest," rejoined the friar. She was soon after condemned to the stake, and endured her punishment with such patience, that her courage caused great admiration.

At Arras, in Artois, there was the chapel of the Holy Candle. There was a candle in it which the priests said, had been sent down from heaven, and was never consumed. The devout used to sing hymns to it. It was the custom to have watchers every day and night around this holy candle. Nicholas, surnamed the *Penman*, heard the story about this wonderful taper, how it never would burn out, and said, "that is what we will see."

"If they would let us be the watchers for a while we might," said two of his friends, who had received from Nicholas much instruction in the gospel. One day they were appointed to keep the watch. They took their station, and were careful not to go to sleep. The priests had no chance to creep in with a new candle, on account of these inquisitive men; an old trick that the superstitious people had never detected. So the perpetual candle came to an end, as might be supposed.

"Come in, you poor idolaters," said Nicholas, the next morning, "and see how the holy light has gone out. There is nothing left but the burnt out wick." As a reward for this discovery, the three Christians received the crown of martyrdom together.

Thus the persecution raged throughout France. "One sees nothing in Paris," wrote a Roman Catholic eye-witness, "but gibbets set up in various places, which surely terrify the people of the said Paris, and those of other places, who also see gallows and executions." Another chronicler says: "But for ten that were put to death, a hundred others sprang up from their ashes."

One winter's day, Calvin saw an old man arrive at Basle; he was half blind, and felt his way as he walked. It was Courault, whom Queen Margaret had freed from the convent, where he had been shut up. It was a great joy to Calvin to see this venerable Christian again. The refugees gathered around him. They wanted to hear the terrible news from Paris. As he described the woes of the faithful, cries of sorrow rose from all who had friends still exposed to the horrors of the stake. Courault was followed by other fugitives. Nicholas Cop was already there, having been for some time on the watch for his friend Calvin.

The true Christian peeple of the towns and cities, where these refugees sought protection, were given to hospitality. At Strasburg, the house of the good pastor, Matthew Zell, was known to all Christian travellers, and especially to the exiles from all lands. He often had a large number of persecuted wanderers around his table every day for weeks. At one time, there came one hundred and fifty men, who had left their homes, at Brisgau, in the middle of the night, and reached the city in great distress. It was night, but Catharine, the pastor's wife, found means to lodge four-score of them in the parsonage, and for a month had nearly sixty of them at her table. She was never weary in well-doing. We may suppose that many an exile from Paris, coming to her door, with the love of Christ in his heart, was welcome to the best that her hands could supply.

Ten years after these events John Calvin was passing through a little town in Switzerland on a very rainy day. At the door of a school-house he saw a man whom he thought he had seen before in Paris. As he often met such former acquaintances, his glance became a fixed gaze. It was returned by the teacher of the school, who asked, "Is this our dear Calvin?"

"Is this my modest Vallette?" was the reply. They spent no short time in their greetings and inquiries.

"You must stop for the day. I will have you talk to my scholars as long as you choose, and dismiss them. Then you will come to my home." Calvin hesitated. "Would you not like to see Jeanne La Forge?"

"Surely; it would be worth a week's lingering in this town."

"You shall see her, and her aged mother, for she

is now Madame Vallette." Calvin addressed the scholars, went to a little cottage, and spent twenty-four of the happiest hours of his life. From their varied experiences, these friends drew fresh commentaries upon the text, "Fear not little flock, for it is your Father's good pleasure to give you the kingdom." They parted with those golden words, "If God be for us, who can be against us?"

THE END.

www.ingramcontent.com/pod-product-compliance
Lightning Source LLC
LaVergne TN
LVHW021402110826
845150LV00007B/1751

* 9 7 8 1 4 2 5 5 1 3 3 5 1 *